This is vintage Bewes – he introduces
takes me to places I've never been, co
fellowship, and all in a lively, move-al
Gospel of Mark! Richard is both ferv
sane. Best of all, it's a book on revival
of it!

Dale Ralph Davis
Minister-in-Residence, First Presbyterian Church,
Columbia, South Carolina

Richard has ransacked the Bible and the nations to provide us
with a bird's-eye (and at times, ring-side) view of those remarkable
periods when we glimpse the powers of the coming age as the Lord
Almighty works in concentrated spiritual revival. He draws us into
his personal passion with theological clarity, historical perspective
and pastoral wisdom. Unsurprisingly, given the author, this book
is, by turns, jaw-dropping, mind-stretching, hope-stirring, heart-
warming and above all, Christ-exalting.

Craig Dyer
Pastor, Harper Church, Glasgow,
International Director of Training for Christianity Explored

This is an inspiring and instructive introduction to revival and
its effects on individuals, on the church and on society. Firmly
based on scripture and illustrated from ancient and contemporary
history of revival, this book also gives sobering accounts of
counterfeit revivals and of genuine revivals attacked and blunted
by faulty theology, self and Satan. The net effect on the reader is
a yearning to experience all that God has prepared for us or more
accurately, as this book emphasises, to experience more of Jesus.
Read it slowly, as I did, and let God minister to you, as he did to me.

Ajith Fernando
Teaching Director, Youth for Christ, Sri Lanka

This is a wonderful example of one generation declaring the Lord's works to another. Simple, yet profound, it is a timely reminder of our need to depend on God in prayer and repentance rather than believing we can manage our way out of the crisis that faces the church today. A book to read, and read again.

Susie Leafe
Director of Reform, Sheffield,
Member of the General Synod of the Church of England

Drawing on his Bible and a life-time of personal experience, Richard takes us to the heart of true revival, brought about by the preaching of the death and resurrection of the Lord Jesus, and leading to transformed lives. He stirs us to prayer and self-examination, and warns us against false manifestations. Along the way, with his hallmark readable style, he encourages us with wonderful and untold (to me at least) stories of the Lord's work around the world. He makes us long to see more of the gospel's advance and reminds us how this really is God's power for salvation.

Alasdair Paine
Vicar, St Andrew the Great, Cambridge,
a director of the Keswick Convention

This book packs a spiritual wallop. Every Christian praying that God would work in great power in our day should read it. Wonderful revival stories conjoined to wise biblical reflections cascade through the volume's pages. These stories testify to the dynamic power of the Gospel of Jesus Christ to transform lives. The author's first-hand participation in revivals, especially in Africa, well qualifies him to write. May this book provide a fresh impulse for Christians worldwide to pray for revival in our Gospel starved communities.

John Woodbridge
Research Professor of Church History and Thought,
Trinity International University, Deerfield, Illinois

Born out of the family's experience of the East African Revival and passionate about seeing such refreshment and renewal again,

Richard Bewes tells the story of God's sovereign work in bringing revival across nations and down the ages. Richard's wealth of biblical wisdom and warmth caused me to plead: 'Do it again, Lord, and start with me!' Do read this book and pray for times of refreshing, renewal and, please God, Revival!

Simon Vibert
Vicar, Christ Church, Virginia Water, Surrey

Written in characteristic easy-to-read Richard Bewes style, the Thorn Tree mixes history, truth and heart-warming stories to clear our heads and excite our hearts about Revival. A great introduction to the subject which should whet your appetite for more.

Hugh Palmer
Rector, All Souls Langham Place, London,
and Honorary Chaplain to the Queen

UNDER THE THE THORN TREE

UNDER THE THORN TREE

WHEN REVIVAL COMES
RICHARD BEWES

CHRISTIAN
FOCUS

CONTENTS

DEDICATION

My warmest thanks to Harvey Thomas CBE who – with his wife Marlies at his side – has graciously written the foreword to this book. And how can I ever thank my dearest wife Pam for her typing and checking abilities? She has shared with me in the putting together of every page and indeed every word of what you are about to read. ...

We dedicate this book, remembering the last wonderful visit we made together to the home, in Montreat, North Carolina, of a beloved man, Dr Billy Graham. Under God he has shaped the lives of us both by his inspired preaching and his warm friendship.

Richard Bewes,
Virginia Water,
Surrey, England   June 2017

FOREWORD

Young and old, two legged and four footed – all Africa gathers around the thorn tree. The umbrella-like acacia tree gives shade, protection and a place to meet, to study, to reflect and to pray! Its shelter acts as town hall, school, community centre and church.

In this marvellous book, Richard's story starts in the early days of the East African Revival when a few believers, going through testing times, sat and prayed with their Bibles open under a thorn tree in Rwanda, and left, fired afresh to take the saving power of Jesus far and wide.

God has blessed Richard Bewes with an amazing array of gifts – preacher, musician, writer, pastor – and story-teller. Born and raised in Kenya, he now has a world-wide ministry through his books and videos. Here in the U.K., the work of African Enterprise also benefits greatly from his experience, his compassion, and his gentle, Christ-centred words of wisdom which invariably both clarify and move us forward – just as he does in *Under the Thorn Tree*.

Every page is a gripping story – and a sermon in itself – always with the clear message that for the believer and the church, revival is the *natural* way – not a special event. Revival starts with *'a few hearts in which a flame has been lit by the Holy Spirit of God'*, in those who talk not about *'revival'* – but about *Jesus*.

As Communications Director for Margaret Thatcher over many years, my task was often to search for true, substantive *'sound bites'* – and in politics that was usually a difficult job. *Under the Thorn Tree* is scattered with short, vivid messages that are so easy to read and understand:

> 'When God is marching on, it seems that he will scrape up anyone who is open to the Call.' 'When the reviving Spirit of the Lord takes over ...'

> 'The Cross for ever remains at the centre of every mighty moving of God's Spirit.' 'The greatest need of the church is to catch a fresh vision of Jesus Christ.'

– and many, many more.

Revival is an integral part of who Richard Bewes is. He radiates Christ and as we read these pages, we feel, almost physically, his burning desire to point the reader back to the 'Power of the Blood' shed by Jesus at Calvary.

For many years Richard has been one of Billy Graham's closest personal friends and confidantes, and he has dedicated this book to him. Among many other roles, Richard was chairman of Billy Graham's 1989 *Mission to London*. I had the privilege of preparing Billy Graham missions around the world for 15 years, and I know personally how deeply Billy has valued their friendship. When he first came to England back in 1954, a journalist accused him of *'putting the church back 50 years'*. Billy's response was, *'I'm disappointed in a way, I was trying to set it back 2,000 years!'* In these chapters, Richard has done just that – taken us back to the person of Jesus Christ as the only essential for true revival.

It is because its author and its content are so totally Christ-centred that *Under the Thorn Tree* is so powerful. In Richard's words it's *'an exciting look back on great revivals – but always from the thrilling story-line of the Bible, and the fire and power of Heaven itself.'*

My wife Marlies and I could never put a value on our friendship with Richard and his lovely Pam – or what they mean to us in our personal lives and in so many professional areas; and it is my privilege to commend this book to you with enormous enthusiasm. As you read it, your spirit will be inspired and challenged by the insight, wisdom and love of Christ that is evidenced in every line.

You will find, as I have done, that *'the whole message is just for me'*.

Harvey Thomas CBE
London, England

1
BORN IN A REVIVAL

'Will you not revive us again,
that your people may rejoice in you?'

(Psalm 85:6)

Revival, eh? There have been numbers of great 'Awakenings' in Christian history when the windows of Heaven seemed to open in an unusual way – with a visitation of God's power and blessing so great that there seemed not enough room to contain it (Mal. 3:10). My long-standing next-door neighbour, Dr John Stott, once suggested to me that no revival was greater than the mighty sixteenth-century Reformation that swept Europe, under the preaching and writing of such giants as Luther, Calvin, Knox – and noble martyrs such as Tyndale, Archbishop Cranmer, Ann Askew, Latimer and Ridley.

But there have been numbers of further awakenings in the last three hundred years, associated with Wesley and Whitefield, Jonathan Edwards, Charles Finney and D.L. Moody; Evan Roberts in Wales, Willie Nicholson of Northern Ireland and Duncan Campbell of the Hebrides.

In the pages ahead, an exciting look-back on these – and many other names and places from around the world – awaits us, but always from the thrilling story-line of the Bible, and the fire and power of Heaven itself. And oh – the stories!

SIX THOUSAND FEET UP!

My own first awareness of God's awakening power was when the East African Revival of the mid-twentieth century touched my early life in Kenya, where I was growing up within the family of our missionary parents, Cecil and Sylvia Bewes.

My parents had first been on the front line of evangelism and church planting in the remote Kenyan area of Kabare, facing – as they were – the animistic beliefs of East Africa, together with the hold that the *mundu-mugo,* the witch doctor, had upon great swathes of people. For them and their African colleagues, it was prayer, the Bible and the steady proclamation of the Cross that would ultimately overthrow the powers of darkness. And revival? As my saintly mother would later laugh, 'Revival couldn't really come to Kabare until after we'd left!'

It was at my second African home, in Weithaga – 6,000 feet up, and on the lower slopes of Mount Kenya – that I first sensed the power of the Cross touch great numbers of people. Under the red corrugated iron roof of our bungalow we were without running water, sanitation, gas or electricity, and there were no shops, doctors or hospitals anywhere within the region. It was only 'Auntie Lorna' – a single missionary of uncertain age – who, though not a qualified nurse, held a somewhat tenuous authority to dispense iodine, bandages and the occasional injection from her minute dispensary nearby.

My dad's missionary car was the only available form of transport. Indeed, within the battered box-body of the Ford V8, a small Kikuyu baby was, one day, prematurely born – and delivered by Dad. Later the grateful mother celebrated the birth by naming her little boy '*Motoka*'.

TROPICAL HAZARDS

It was inevitable that I would grow up bilingual, and even to this day I can sing you 'Blessed Assurance' in the Kikuyu dialect! Certain care had to be negotiated against a variety of tropical hazards. Before the development of pesticides, vast locust swarms – fifty miles in length – would sweep down from the Middle East along East Africa's great Rift Valley. The sky could become black as night, as umpteen million of the voracious insects descended on the fields and crops. We would hear the branches of trees cracking under their weight. Car drivers had to stop when their windscreens became blotted out. I can recall seeing my dad vainly trying to beat off a terrifying swarm with the aid of a single tennis racket. How my heart swelled with pride in him!

Or there were the *siafu* – the 'safari ants,' which would devour anything living in their path as they marched in solid ranks through villages and homesteads. Oh, the shock, when one morning it was discovered that a line of ants had gone through our hen house, and had entirely consumed a single hen sitting dutifully upon her eggs, leaving only a bare skeleton behind. 'Jiggers' (in the toes) and tarantulas (in the shoes) had to be reckoned with, while poisonous puff adders could be a menace to livestock and humans. Coming out of our back veranda one day, I heard the husky hiss of a black mamba just two feet behind me, where it nestled in the shade. Whirling round, I saw its head rearing up – and I ran for my life. It took a band of experienced African friends, armed with long pointed poles, to dispatch the venomous six-foot snake.

Yet all this we seemed to take in our stride; this was Africa! No child could have had a calmer upbringing, educated as we were by my mother on the side veranda of our missionary home that is still in existence.

Some miles away rolled the Maragua river, and Dad would sometimes take us fishing for trout in the icy waters that flowed out of the glaciers of Mount Kenya. On one such expedition, Dad shot a python that was strangling a small impala, and for some years the python's skin served as a gruesome reminder along the whole length of the veranda.

REVIVAL IN WEITHAGA

With Bible stories every night, together with readings from Kipling's *Just So Stories* and Bunyan's *Pilgrim's Progress*, the Revival – when it descended upon Weithaga – was to me the most natural occurrence that could ever have happened. It fitted in completely with the umpteen stories from the Scriptures that had slowly been building my own boyhood understanding of the meaning of life on this world.

But naturally – with the infusion of new life from Above – there were crowds! On Sundays we would go down to the sizeable church developed by my dad, but there would be no room to contain the vast numbers. The grass around the church would have to be beaten down – for fear of snakes – before anything could begin. Then the drums would start to roll, and the preaching would begin! During the great Christian festivals, the crowds were uncountable; was it four thousand, six thousand … even eight thousand? At Harvest time, numerous sticks of sugar cane, great bunches of bananas, flapping poultry – and even live goats – would be joyfully brought to church by grateful worshippers. Our African neighbours loved singing at the best of times, and on any day we would hear the songs of the Gospel as they echoed across the valleys and hills of the Kikuyu Highlands. Lives were changed and testimonies abounded in the frequent 'fellowship meetings' attended by those who were being touched by the remarkable awakening.

One day a man came to our door.

'I have come,' he said, 'because Jesus has come into my life and I am here to bring you restitution.'

'Restitution?' said Dad. 'Whatever do you mean?'

'Ah,' came the reply, 'you would never have known. But I used to sell you eggs, here at the front door, and I have to tell you that for many months I was first going round to the back of your house where you keep your chickens, and I was stealing the eggs laid by your hens … and bringing them round to the front door to sell you your own eggs! I have repented, by the Blood of Jesus, and that's why I'm here.'

Stories like this abounded. With the renewed emphasis on the saving Gospel of Christ, evangelism became a priority. One day a Mission was announced at Weithaga. The church elders were thrilled at the prospect and sent word out around the locality, giving a date for its beginning. They even agreed unanimously to announce the Preacher for the event.

'There's one man, surely, whom we want ... and it's Mwangi. It is going to be him!'

But then, where was Mwangi to be found? Emails, telephones – and even the post – were light years away as far as Weithaga was concerned. Runners were sent out to locate Mwangi, but no word came back. The day of the Mission's opening drew ever nearer, and anxiety began to set in. Where was our gifted Kikuyu preacher? But finally, on the very first day of the Mission, Mwangi turned up.

'Oh, Mwangi – praise God! So word got to you then?'

'Word? What word? I never got any message.'

'Why – we've sent out messengers everywhere to look for you! Where have you been all this time?'

'Oh,' came the reply, 'I've been out in the bush, having some quiet days with the Lord. But only this morning the Lord seemed to be saying to me, "Mwangi, you must go now. They are needing you at Weithaga!"'

This was the atmosphere of the Spirit-led community that I was becoming accustomed to – and it was very African. There came the day when – from the centre of the Revival – there arrived in Weithaga two inspiring evangelists, whose speaking had been signally blessed in Rwanda and Uganda; Simeoni Nsibambi and Yosiya Kinuka. One day, Dad remarked on the fact that Simeoni went everywhere in bare feet, and Dad asked, 'Why? We'd be glad enough to get you some shoes, if that would help.'

'Not for me,' replied the evangelist. 'Shoes are good – but having grown up from the beginning without them, I have to tell you that every time I put shoes on my feet, I could sense pride welling up in my heart, and – coming as I do from a simple background – I prefer to stay as I am, lest I become conceited!'

'I understand,' came the reply. Then Dad pointed at Simeoni's companion. 'But what about Yosiya, then? We can see that he wears shoes!'

'Yes, he does,' agreed Simeoni. *'But he's taken them out of his heart!'*

And that, indeed, is what seems to happen to motives and actions, when the reviving Spirit of the Lord takes over.

EMERGENCY IN KENYA

Furthermore – the long-standing African resentment against colonial domination by white Europeans became tempered by the spirit of understanding and love that the Cross brings to a community of believers. It was not that the Christians of Kenya were any less desirous of political independence than their neighbours. But violence could never be the name of the game – as happened when the notorious 'Mau Mau' terrorist organization came into being, primarily among the Kikuyu – with its aim of overthrowing white supremacy by violence.

Soon it became clear that the main force of the Mau Mau attack was against those who were supposedly the 'loyal' Kikuyu. 'Get these traitors out of the way first,' declared the Mau Mau, 'then we can finish off the Europeans.'

Huts were barricaded, thatch was set on fire, and Kikuyu Christians were hacked to death as they ran outside – or burnt alive if they remained within. Their 'crime' lay in their refusal to take the Mau Mau oath which was enforced with pagan blood sacrifices. The solemn, yet inspiring fact was that the vast bulk of refusals to accept the terrorist oath were made by the *saved ones* of the Revival Fellowship. 'We can never partake of this pagan blood,' they would say, 'we who, by the New Birth and at the Holy Communion, have shared in the Precious Blood of Jesus.'

The killings were numerous. One appalling massacre occurred in the village of Lari the very day after Dad had sat and ministered among scores of men, women and children as they shared from the Scriptures, singing, and praising together.

My dad would eventually join *The Fairn Commission*, set up from London to begin the moves towards Kenya's political independence. Before then, he had written in his book 'Kikuyu Conflict': *This is the most thrilling fellowship that ever I met in my life, a fellowship that surpasses all the barriers of colour and race. The Mau Mau were trusting in the blood of a pagan sacrifice, the Revival brethren found the perfect answer in the Blood shed once for all on Calvary, ever available for cleansing and pardon and peace. We have nothing else to trust in, nothing else to boast about, there is no other righteousness for any of us, no other fountain for sin – nothing but the Blood of Jesus'.[1]

Jealousies, rivalries, personal grudges and pride become banished under the power of Heaven. No room can be left for any form of competition or 'empire building' within a true Gospel fellowship. This represents a massively needed message for Christians in the West.

But before we can touch on this, let us benefit from the stories of how revivals can begin. The next pages will bring Simeoni and Yosiya back into view again as we see them

---

[1] T.F.C. Bewes, *Kikuyu Conflict: Mau Mau and the Christian Witness* (London: The Highway Press, 1953).

grouped with their colleagues, together with one of my dad's college friends from England; an earnest group sitting together with their Bibles open under a thorn tree ...

'The Revival has made it real for some of us all over again, for we can see in it our only hope, our only ground for confidence.'[2]

2 T.F.C. Bewes

2

UNDER THE THORN TREE

*'A revival always includes conviction of
sin on the part of the Church.'*[1]

It was the end of a Sunday at All Souls Church in London
as I stood at the exit and greeted a young Ugandan woman.

'Do tell me your name,' I said.

'My name is Rose Nsibambi.'

I froze. *'Nsibambi?'* I echoed. 'Oh my – do you have
any connection with a wonderful evangelist called Simeoni
Nsibambi?'

'He was my grandfather,' came the reply.

I stared, mesmerized, hardly knowing what to say.
If I could have done anything, I would have knelt at the
young woman's feet. For the name *Simeoni Nsibambi* represented a man completely unknown along the corridors
of sophisticated society, but whose name is surely written
in the Book of God. It was he who would one day – in
Uganda's capital, Kampala – appeal for Christian counsel

---

1 Charles Finney: *Lectures on Revival* (USA: Bethany House Publishers).

14

and fellowship with Dr. Joe Church, an English medical missionary, who had studied with my dad at Emmanuel College Cambridge. For days, Simeoni and Joe met and studied their Bibles, as they lamented over their own sins and the spiritual desolation of East Africa.

AT THE LOWEST EBB

Earlier on, Joe – who would become a kind of 'uncle missionary' to me – had already been agonizing over the desperate conditions in the country of Rwanda. He had started his own hospital at Gahini, with a team that included his able hospital dresser, Yosiya Kinuka. But the early months proved to be a nightmare, following the failure of the rains, the onset of famine, and the presence of numerous refugees around the mission hospital. Dysentery was rife, and the churches were crippled by the nominal Christianity that prevailed everywhere. Unannounced, some of Joe's best staff – in their own despondency – had walked out. Joe was at his lowest ebb, crushed by sin and failure. We cannot be too precise as to when the East African Revival actually began. When the power of Heaven is released in the reviving of the church, the Spirit of God works in His sovereign authority, as and where He determines. The effect – as Jesus said to a seeking Pharisee, Nicodemus – is not unlike the wind which seems to blow wherever it will (John 3:8). In the Welsh Revival of 1904, the blessing of churches and whole villages seemed to be occurring almost at random, as the entire country came under the wind of God.

There are indeed variously-told beginnings of the East African Revival. However, we can instance the experience of Dr. Joe Church as providing for us, perhaps, the most well-known account.

NDERA'S 'UMBRELLA TREE'

The first change came in September 1929, when 'Uncle' Joe
climbed Ndera Hill, some ten miles from Rwanda's capital,
Kigali. There he sat in the shade of what he called 'an
umbrella tree', with the morning mist beginning to break
over a nearby lake. As Patricia St John records: *'He prayed
passionately for the scattering of the mists of superstition
and sin, and the shining forth of the light of the Gospel …
and the sight of the beautiful spreading acacia tree seemed
like holy ground to be claimed for God. Something had
happened to him under that old acacia tree.'*[2]

It was only days later, when climbing Kampala's
Namirembe Hill, that Simeoni Nsibambi was to confront
Joe Church with his request to meet. As the two men sat
and prayed together – consulting their Bibles incessantly –
conviction and hope began to stir within.

The time would come when Joe was once again under
the thorn tree at Ndera; this time accompanied by his
hospital dresser, Yosiya, and by other team members –
including Simeoni's younger half-brother, Blasio Kigozi, a
young evangelist blazing with fervour. It was December
1934, as the group gazed over the country below and
thought of the many thousands of people in such need of
Christ's gospel. Two days after Christmas they assembled
a *safari* team for a whole journey of 150 miles on foot, into
a literally barren mission field. As Joe was to write: 'It was
the first time that *'Jesus loves me'* and *'There is a happy
land'* had pierced the silence of those hills and valleys.'

---

2 Patricia St John, *Breath of Life* (UK: Norfolk Press, 1971) p. 67.

PREACHING TEAMS

The momentum began to pick up – despite the shock, shortly after, of the unexpected death by fever of Blasio Kigozi. Nevertheless Simeoni was becoming well known in Kampala and beyond; forever in bare feet and carrying his well-worn Bible. Outgoing teams of preachers were dramatically effective as they spread the message of Christ crucified, of the new birth and the indwelling Holy Spirit's empowering of the new believer for immediate public witness. Confession of sin, restitution and frequent apology were becoming common. Beer drinking was losing its appeal, and many were stirred enough to walk many miles in order to mend a relationship or indeed to ask a pastor, 'What must I do to be saved?'

Unusual manifestations have very frequently occurred in the exciting wake of a true revival. At one point when the Revival swept through a Ugandan farmland, the cry went up, 'Look, there is fire on the backs of the cattle!' That same night many felt an urge to go to the darkened church to pray – only to find at the top of the hill that the church itself was glowing with a soft light. Others too seemed to hear a voice summoning them to come, as they weepingly arrived through the darkness to seek God. Frequently – during church services – men would fall on their faces in their confession of sin, followed immediately by cries of joy as they accepted God's forgiveness.

Naturally, in the wake of open testimonies, mass weeping, the dreaming of dreams or prolonged singing of hymns into the early hours, the hackles could rise – from those rooted in established nominalism, and indeed from numbers of the church hierarchy, including European missionaries, theologians and clergy. There would inevitably

be those who described revival manifestations as hinder-
ing the ongoing stability of the church! There were indeed
gifted revival evangelists who – on their request to enter
theological training for ordination – were flatly turned
down by the authorities. Among them was one of the most
effective evangelists that Africa has ever known, Uganda's
William Nagenda.

The redoubtable theologian Max Warren inserted a
sane comment in his book *Revival – an Enquiry*.[3] '*Revival
is a perilous experience,*' he wrote. '*But the perils of revival
must be set beside the perils of Laodicea.*' For Laodicea –
the last of the seven churches described in the book of
Revelation – accurately described the 'lukewarm' life of
many churches in Europe and the West.

'SECTARIAN' QUESTIONS

A vital issue was to arise: '*Is the revival movement a sect?*'
The question can stem from the common inclination to
build a phantom picture of any great new movement. Ultimately this happens when the general focus is on the workers, or 'heroes', instead of fastening on to Christ Himself
and the life of His church. We will reserve for another
chapter the question of where the true centre of a revival
occurs. But it should not be too surprising that Pentecostal
joy can sometimes overspill in ways that the cold nominalism of Laodicea would have recoiled from.

The great triumph of the East African awakening was
that it was very largely owned and kept within the life of the
Church and its local fellowships. Had that not happened,
the movement would have become splintered in the general

---

3 Max Warren, *Revival – An Enquiry* (London: SCM Press, 1954).

tribal tensions and jealousies that all too often have tended to mar the national well-being of the sunlit countries within the African continent. Despite certain split-offs, the Revival as a whole was to produce men and women of great leadership and calibre – and the Church worldwide was benefited. The West today finds itself drawing strength from inspired bishops – and indeed archbishops and other leaders in Protestant leadership – right across from West Africa, through to the Congo and on to the East African coast. Worry not whether these spirit-led leaders are from Yuroba, Igbo, Hausa – or indeed from the Kikuyu, Luwo or even the one-time warlike Masai tribes – we seem not to find a trace of any liberal unbelief among them!

There is something else we must recognise. In any major revival – from Pentecost onwards – no 'big' names ever predominated. True, in any century, the world may be lifted by a single outstanding and gifted evangelist, seemingly able to move mountains ... and the Christian Church breathes more easily.

There was the 'golden-mouthed preacher of Constantinople', John Chrysostom. Europe was changed through the preaching of Martin Luther. We have had William Grimshaw of Yorkshire, Jonathan Edwards and Charles Finney of New England, Willie Nicholson of Ireland – not to mention D.L. Moody of Chicago, and Billy Graham of North Carolina. But even of these last two – who would become known worldwide – it must be acknowledged that Moody (whose last letter contained no less than thirty-six spelling mistakes) was drawn from his work at a shoe-maker's bench, while Billy Graham grew up as a farmer's boy in Charlotte.

WHAT ARE THE CREDENTIALS?

In the earliest days of the Church, we read of the astonishment exhibited by the opponents of the new Jesus movement as they met Peter and John, and realized 'that they were unschooled, ordinary men' (Acts 4:13). It seems typical of the Lord that, when He included members of the Israeli fishing industry among His apostles, He was only underlining what had been long ordained – that when it comes to identifying the 'use-able' among us, *God looks upon the heart*. Back in the Old Testament, the choice for *a judge* fell on Gideon, busy on his threshing floor; for *a prophet* – on Amos, as he ploughed his field; for *a king* – on David, as he tended the sheep; for *a governor* – on Nehemiah, butler to a pagan despot. The glory of God is never to be hi-jacked!

> 'Brothers and sisters, think of what you were when you were called. Not many of you were wise by human standards; not many were influential; not many of you were of noble birth. But God chose the foolish things of the world to shame the wise; God chose the weak things of the world to shame the strong. God chose the lowly things of this world and the despised things – and the things that are not – to nullify the things that are, so that no one may boast before him' (1 Cor. 1:26-29).

So … for an evangelist, let us take Yosiya Kinuka, a local hospital dresser in Gahini! Let us take Simeoni Nsibambi, a sixteen-year-old footballer and wrestler studying at Uganda's Mengo High School! Let us take Joe Church, a shortish man with a little moustache, who will have to try and improve his public speaking!

About this last-named, most people could only agree. No one ever described Joe Church as a powerful, dominating personality, with a gift for words. To me, who first met him out in East Africa, he seemed little more than a useful hockey player; friendly, indeed – and always approachable – but just 'Uncle Joe'. I recall – when later studying at university in the U.K. – that we were urged by the leader of the Christian Union to attend what he called 'A Missionary Breakfast'.

'And there's going to be a speaker,' he announced, 'a man from the great East African Revival, and you've all got to hear him! He's a man filled with the Holy Ghost!'

We all looked at one other timorously. Umm. Filled with the Holy Ghost! Can we cope? ... And then, 'Uncle Joe' turned up – *Oh – Dad's old college hockey-playing chum!* Was that it, then?

And that precisely *is* It. Think of Joe Church, alone underneath that 'Umbrella' acacia tree – then joined by others in their quest for God's cleansing and awakening in the Spirit. Eventually a church was to be built around that historic thorn tree. Can you see them there? Join them if you will, as – like them – your heart beats with others for heaven's windows to open and the rains to fall!

*'I feel I am looking through a window
into somewhere far ahead, like someone dreaming.
I see Christ coming towards me... .'*

(BLASIO KIGOZI, 8 AUGUST 1935 –
BEFORE HIS DEATH AT GAHINI)

3

HEARTS, BEATING AS ONE

'The world is waking out of a long deep sleep.'

(LETTER FROM THE REFORMER ERASMUS
TO SIR HENRY GUILDFORD, MAY 1519)

Residents of the English county of Hampshire may know
the story of the ancient yew tree in the village of Selbourne. It had been planted fourteen hundred years
ago. Across the centuries, the tree had outlasted the Nor-
man conquest of Britain in 1066, the Battle of Agincourt
against the French in 1415, and by the time of King Henry VIII, the yew tree was nearly a thousand years old.
The tree continued through the years of the Reformation,
England's Civil War, the battles with Napoleon, the War
of American Independence, and – later still – Roosevelt,
Churchill, Hitler, Stalin, Mao Tse Tung, Gorbachev ...
and Thatcher.

   And then one night – in the great storm of 25th
January, 1990 – the Selbourne Yew first tottered and then,
unbelievably, fell. People passing by the next day could

scarcely believe what they saw. It had always been there, and now ... it had gone.

I take the moving story of the Selbourne Yew as sym-bolical of what can sometimes appear to happen to entire peoples and their belief-systems.

DECISIVE CROSSROADS

The prophet Jeremiah was faced with a similar collapse in the seventh century B.C. *'This is what the Lord says,'* he announced: *'Stand at the crossroads and look; ask for the ancient paths, ask where the good way is and walk in it, and you will find rest for your souls. But you said, 'We will not walk in it''* (Jer. 6:16).

The question raised itself: whatever had happened to Israel's long-standing covenant relationship with the Lord? It had begun centuries earlier with Abraham; strengthened through Moses, battled for by Joshua, defended by Samuel, celebrated by David ... and vindicated by Elijah, Amos and Isaiah. What had become of this massive, divine emblem of secure permanence by the time of Jeremiah? It had always been there! Now – to all appearances – it was about to go.

We could ask the same thing of the Christianity that once seemed so firmly rooted – and familiar to all of us in the West. We had enjoyed the language and terms of the Bible in common use, the establishing of spires and chapels everywhere. We had seen the epic of the Reforma-tion; we had been blessed by the writings of Bunyan, the preaching of Spurgeon, the awakenings under Wesley and Whitefield, Jonathan Edwards, Torrey, and Moody. We had been bolstered by the triumph of the Sunday schools, the rock-face of Marriage and the hold that the Christian Sunday has always had upon the West.

But to outward observation it now appears that – though the Christian faith once seemed forever to be securely rooted and embedded in our society, spreading its protective shade over education, marriage and the law-making of western nations – it is now, at least in the mindset of the media and the institutions, *gone* ... and for some, indeed, might never have been.

Jeremiah's words speak right into his own era, and in fact into any period where destructive powers have done their worst in removing the one mighty understanding of life that lifts a civilization.

TWO ARE ENOUGH

In taking up Jeremiah's summons, we should try to re-live the entrancing story of two young hearts that beat together ... for revival! For that is how spiritual awakenings tend to be born – not through imposing committees or resounding resolutions, but simply through a few hearts in which a flame has been lit by the Holy Spirit of God.

It was in 639 B.C. – the year of Jeremiah's birth – that another little boy was born near Jerusalem, by the name of Josiah. He was to become king, astonishingly, at the age of eight.

Jeremiah and Josiah; both boys grew up in Jerusalem, both knew the Lord, and both were committed in their call to service – although while Josiah was brave and fear-less, Jeremiah could shake and quiver at what he would be required to do.

Two young lives; the new king – and a future proph-et ... and at the age of twenty, young King Josiah began a campaign to bring the people back to God. A major impetus was given to the revival with the discovery in

Jerusalem's Temple of a pack of dust-laden parchments that turned out to be the five books of Moses that had been lost – centuries back, perhaps under the rule of wicked King Manasseh.

With their discovery, Hilkiah the priest went white with excitement as he gasped, 'I have found the book of the law!' (2 Chron. 34:15)

Here was the very missing copy of the first five books of the Bible. Breathlessly, the parchments were put into the hands of young King Josiah – who, as he began to read them, ripped his jacket with grief. 'We've completely failed our God,' he began to cry. 'Let's come back to the Lord again, and let's hold Passovers once more! We've got to get back to the ancient paths!'

Meanwhile, Jeremiah had begun his own preaching around the streets. His call to preach came when he was just a thirteen-year-old. A little young, perhaps, for such a call?

But no; the earlier, the better! Here then are these two boys. King Josiah, now aged twenty-one, cleaning up the land – and Jeremiah, the boy preacher. Both were lovers of the Lord, and not altogether unlike John and Charles Wesley, centuries later, who as young men would resolve, *By God's grace, we are going to change the course of history!*

THE BOILING CAULDRON

True, it would be a big burden, where Jeremiah himself was concerned. One day, the people would turn on him. He would be imprisoned. He would be thrown into a deep, muddy pit – but even there the Lord would say to him, 'Don't be afraid.' As we know from the Scriptures,

his preaching would be lit up with inspired visions. He
spoke of a boiling cauldron, about to tip over; a vivid reminder to his listeners that there was still time to avert
the judgment of God, if they would only return to *the old
paths* – and repent.

We are faced today by plenty of church leaders who, in
their abject desertion of biblical centralities, will exclaim,
'No, no – we've moved *on* now!' If Jeremiah was alive today, he would surely counter such revisionists by saying,
'The only sure way to move *on* is to move *back* – to the
old, trusted paths, trodden by a long convoy of faithful
heralds!'

Here then were Jeremiah and Josiah – two men only –
fired by the same call and the same concern. Can we take
it in? *There's power in that.* Two people are enough!

In a terrible blow, Josiah was eventually killed in battle at the age of thirty-eight, and Jeremiah was to manage alone, in his urgent call to repentance. It surely took
courage to keep on ministering, while facing a coalition of
the kings, the officials, the priests and indeed the people
themselves.

This is precisely where we are in the church of the West
at the present time. Yet, in Jeremiah's words lie the secret
of a true revival that could spread across a nation.

*'Stand at the crossroads and look; ask for the ancient
paths, ask where the good way is, and walk in it, and you
will find rest for your souls.'*

If we equate the church in the West with the Selbourne
yew tree, we may certainly appear to be tottering towards
collapse, but we must take note of the prophet's four words
of command:

STAND! … AT THE CROSSROADS

'Stop! Stand still! Take stock!' was the message. God's people were indeed at the crossroads of their destiny twenty-six hundred years ago. Eventually Jeremiah would witness the deportation of thousands of his fellow citizens to Babylon, under Nebuchadnezzar. He could see it coming; why could no one else? His message became disastrously fulfilled in his final words: '*… But you said, "We will not walk in it."*'

Where are the faithful ones who can stand still long enough to discern that we may be at the crossroads? Sometimes it takes a personal crisis for men and women to realize the hollowness of society's present corporate dislocation from life and its meaning. Asked for his interpretation of the meaning of life, the atheist Richard Dawkins could only answer in terms of 'the progress of DNA'. Try that, on a village in Haiti, or in a Masai dwelling by Kenya's Ngong Hills, or indeed on a patient waking up in the coronary care unit!

Stop … Stand still … Take stock … ! We are to consider the times we live in. And secondly the word was:

LOOK! …

Jeremiah's listeners were to *look* – not only at their sinful disregard of the Lord, but also at His saving power. This 'looking' is essential. It was sixteen-year-old Charles Spurgeon, one January morning in 1850, who was sitting at the back of a Primitive Methodist Chapel in Colchester, wretched and depressed, when the text was announced by a novice preacher: '*Look unto me, and be ye saved, all the ends of the earth: for I am God, and there is none else*' (Isa. 45:22 KJV). Nothing else could Spurgeon remember, but the text – repeated many times by the stumbling preacher. That was enough. He returned home, utterly transformed in spirit. Here began the call of one of the most inspiring preachers ever to bless the church.

'There is life for a look at the crucified one ...' So runs the first line of a gospel hymn written by Amelia Hull in 1832, on the very night of her accepting Christ as Lord and Saviour.

And ... thirdly:

ASK! ...

'Ask for the ancient paths;' declared the prophet; *'ask where the good way is ...'*

The soil is well prepared for the coming of revival, when there is a yearning in the hearts of God's people. And this – not for a fresh *new* teaching, or an exciting new emphasis – *so much as a coming back to the proven ways of old.* They are the ways proclaimed by a long parade of faithful witnesses, from Noah – that primeval preacher of righteousness – right through a convoy of messengers, prophets and apostles ... and on through such faithful proclaimers as Patrick of Ireland, Torrey of New Jersey and William Nagenda of Uganda.

To ask is to *pray.* On D.L. Moody's first visit to England in 1872, the evangelist regretted having preached on the Sunday morning in front of a sleepy congregation. But a woman there hurried back to her bed-ridden sister and broke the news that Mr. Moody of America had preached.

'I know what that means!' cried her sister, Mary-Anne Adlard. 'God has heard my prayers!' She pulled out from under her pillow a faded newspaper report of Moody's work in Chicago that had prompted her to pray, day after day, 'Lord, send this man one day to our church!' The two women gave the rest of the day to prayer. That evening, when Moody preached again, the meeting seemed charged with Gospel electricity, and within days 400 people were immediately added to the membership of the church. As Moody's biographer wrote, 'it was *then* that the visit to Britain got out of hand.'

Two praying women – that can be enough! Indeed, it was – again – two praying women, aged 82 and 84, whom God used to begin the remarkable Hebrides Revival in November 1949. Appalled at the state of their parish, they began to pray fervently. Then a regular prayer meeting began in a nearby barn – to which hundreds would be drawn ... and a mighty revival resulted.

Stand, Look, Ask – but finally:

WALK! ...

This is the final test of a movement of God! What has it done to character, public behaviour and ethics? The vital call is to refuse all diversions or exciting lay-bys – and to keep on walking along the ancient paths, on the Good Way that by the reviving Spirit of God has been opened up to thousands of God's people.

In the plan of God, His church, like the Selbourne Yew, may become battered in the storms of any and every century, but – by His reviving power – it has never actually been brought down. It never will.

> *'One cannot organize a revival;*
> *it is mysterious as the wind.'*[1]

---

1 Patricia St John, *Breath of Life* (Norfolk Press, 1971).

4

THE HEAVEN-SENT HALLMARKS

*'Most Christians today are unfamiliar with
the big picture principles of revival.'*[1]

There were times, at Cambridge University, when for students to study theology as a preparation for Christian ministry was to enter a spiritual wilderness – negative and arid. Nevertheless many were to remember one of the twentieth-century missions announced by the Cambridge Inter-Collegiate Christian Union (CICCU). The invited preacher for the occasion was none other than the fiery 'tornado of the pulpit' from Bangor, Northern Ireland, Willie Nicholson, who pulled no punches as he lashed out in his deep Irish brogue against the established view that Christianity was merely a matter of following the example of Christ. Totally unused to British universities, his style and manners were so unconventional that many students came to hear him simply to laugh.

On one night Nicholson referred to his unbelieving aunt – and exclaimed, 'She died – and then went straight to

---

1 Tom Phillips, *Jesus Now: God is Up to Something Big* (Broadstreet Publishing, 2016).

hell!' A minute or two later two students decided to make their escape. Nicholson saw them leaving, and shouted after them, 'And if you also ignore the challenge of Christ, you too will go to hell!' Whereupon one of the couple turned around and shouted back, 'Any message for your aunt?' The rest was lost in the general roar of laughter that followed.

Nevertheless, the revival preacher was not afraid of anybody in the stark boldness of his exhortations. The President of the University's Drunks' Club was dramatically converted during Willie's mission – and was later to become secretary of a British missionary society. Night after night there were those who made a profession of faith ... and Willie Nicholson never made it easy for his listeners.

PRAYER BREEDS BRAVERY

From the beginning, *bravery* was the requirement of men and women engaged in proclaiming the good news of Jesus Christ. When the apostles Peter and John were forbidden by the authorities in Jerusalem ever to speak again in the name of Jesus, a prayer meeting was held by their supporters! Had we been among them, we might have felt justified in praying, 'Oh God, may this ban be reversed; may these fires of opposition abate!' Yet in this case the main request of the prayer meeting amounted to, '*Now, Lord, consider their threats, and enable your servants to speak your word with great boldness*' (Acts 4:29). This meant, 'More of the same please!' We read on, that as the prayer meeting closed, 'the place where they were meeting was shaken, and they were all filled with the Holy Spirit and spoke the word of God boldly.'

Not for a moment should the case be made for copying the style of any one preacher. We may have our Willy

Nicholsons to be sure, but the Holy Spirit has manifestly used other preachers noted for the steadiness of their quiet delivery. Pam and I can both remember the utterly compelling way in which the Baptist revival preacher – Stanley Voke, of Upton Vale Church in Torquay – could bring a great hall of listeners to a stunned responsive silence.

It must be emphasized that revival can never be 'worked up'. Rather it is 'sent down,' albeit with preaching as a handmaid to the sovereign action of the Holy Spirit.

The glowing hallmarks of history's revivals can indeed be identified in several ways.

THERE IS HEARTFELT REPENTANCE AND RESTITUTION

The words of John Bunyan, the writer of *Pilgrim's Progress*, are needed in our churches today! 'How many there are,' he wrote, 'who get into churches and obtain the title of brother, a saint, a member of the gospel congregation, *that have clean escaped repentance.*'

More strident was John the Baptist as he addressed the 'brood of vipers' who were listening to him. The crowd asked him, 'What can we do to repent?'

Do? replies the preacher. I'll tell you what to do: 'The man with two tunics should share with him who has none, and the one who has food should do the same!'

The tax collectors then came up. 'What should *we* do?' John replies, 'Don't collect any more than you are required to.'

Now it's the turn of the army soldiers. 'And what shall *we* do?' John knows exactly what to say: 'Don't extort money and don't accuse people falsely – and be content with your pay' (Luke 3:7-14).

Got it? Here were three different ways of expressing repentance ... *And every single one of them was economic.*

Willie Nicholson himself had been a sailor, and at the Belfast shipyard where he ministered there became known 'The Nicholson Shed'. In it were stored the many engineering tools and devices, formerly stolen and now returned by new believers working at the shipyard.

Instances of such restitution can be multiplied. When Revival began in East Africa's Tanzania – the restoration of thousands of stolen axes, saws, hammers and agricultural instruments brought dumbfounded amazement to the government.

The issue of repentance is axiomatic. Over a century ago, C.H. Spurgeon was to sum up the moral shallowness of his own generation when he caustically observed, 'Instead of quitting sin and mourning over it, some men talk of praying!'

THERE IS IMPASSIONED PREACHING OF THE CROSS

'Do you want to get into the attack on the enemy camp in your area? Do you want to exercise the greatest power in the community?'

The speaker was Festo Kivengere, first brought into the life of the Christian church when he was a herd boy, looking after the cattle on a hill in Uganda. We must wait for the next chapter before learning how he became one of the most effective evangelists in the world.

On this occasion, however, it was as an experienced leader in the Revival that he was speaking on the subject, 'Love is a Time Bomb'. *'This power,'* declared Festo, *'is 'Calvary Love' and when we are in fellowship with the risen Christ, day by day, we have a time bomb at our disposal! Nothing has ever succeeded more in ousting the Devil than the love of Calvary.'*

Yet, resistance to the message could be intensively protracted. 'In one region,' reflected Festo, 'the doors were shut against us repeatedly. Our African pastor got into the pulpit one day, and talked of those who preached salvation through the Cross, as "wolves in sheep's clothing". He boomed out, "This is my last warning! If any of you become involved with this message, I will excommunicate you." I and my companions said nothing, but I was feeling bitter. Then the Lord spoke to me: *"You owe deep love to that man. Go to his church, and love him all you can."* So we persisted.

'Then one day the pastor stood before his congregation and wept. "Months ago," he said, "I told you that I would excommunicate any of you who became involved in this message they were talking about. *But I have become saved.* Now you can excommunicate *me* if you like!"'

The Cross of Golgotha has seemed to many people a dead dry thing of the long distant past – but not so to the millions who have embraced its message and accepted God's love. One of our great hymns describes the Cross as, *'His people's hope, His people's wealth, their everlasting theme.'* The Cross forever remains at the centre of every mighty moving of God's Spirit.

We shall look at the Cross again, in a later chapter. Here, however, we can consider a further revival hallmark:

THERE IS WIDESPREAD INTERCESSORY PRAYER

Dr Tom Phillips, of Charlotte, North Carolina, writes of the four Great Awakenings that have touched the nation of America between 1730 and 1940 during the last three hundred and fifty years. Of the third such Awakening (1857–1859) he writes of how ten thousand business men in New York City were gathering in groups for daily prayer, in a movement almost totally led by lay persons. He continues: 'We can only trust that when our nation reaches a point of spiritual, moral and social no-return – as it appeared to do at least three distinct times in history – an extraordinary movement of God's Spirit may move in extraordinary ways in response to prayer for God's broken, contrite children.'[2]

THE KOREAN REVIVAL

In his book *The Korean Revival*, René Monod writes of his first encounter with a prayer meeting during the revival in the city of Seoul. The Korean War had ended. Arriving at five o'clock in the morning, and in the freezing cold, he later wrote, 'My eyes nearly popped out of my head – the whole place was crammed with people. "How many people are there present?" I enquired.

"Almost 3,000 – the whole congregation." I felt dazed, and asked no more questions.'[3]

We may think that praying together represents a kind of 'coalition' before the Lord God. But a coalition is little more than a convenient collaboration between differing parties, in the hope that 'political' pressure might be brought to bear upon a situation. Some might imagine that by sheer force of numbers and voices we can bend God's will to ours! But praying together expresses not a coalition, but an underlying unity of those bonded

---

2 Tom Phillips, *Jesus Now: God is Up to Something Big* (Broadstreet Publishing, 2016).
3 René Monod, *Korean Revival* (UK: Hodder and Stoughton, 1971).

together solely for the interests of Jesus Christ. No special
form or programme is required!

'*Five words, a few broken sentences from a broken
and contrite heart, are more desirable than to pray for
hours without spiritual feeling.*'[4]

THERE IS AN UPLIFT IN PUBLIC MORALITY

Here is a fourth hallmark. In his book on *England*,
covering the years 1870–1914, the radical historian R.C.K.
Ensor commented that no one will understand nineteenth-
century England who doesn't understand the influence
of its evangelical revival in the late eighteenth century;
not least as exercised by the reforming Christian group,
popularly dubbed *The Clapham Sect*.

He wrote, 'If one asks how nineteenth-century English
merchants earned the reputation of being the most honest
in the world (a very real factor in the prominence of English trade), the answer is: because hell and heaven seemed
as certain to them as tomorrow's sunrise; and the Last
Judgment as real as the week's balance sheet.'

Ensor went on to say that the other side of this moral
accountancy was the belief that this life is only important
as a preparation for the next, 'for Evangelicalism made
other-worldliness an every-day conviction, and induced a
highly civilized people to put duty before pleasure to a
quite amazing degree.'[5]

In his own book *John Venn and the Clapham Sect*,
Michael Hennell writes that the members of this highly
motivated band of business men – together with godly

---

4 John Newton, *The Searcher of Hearts* ed. Marylynn Rouse (Tain: Christian
   Focus Publications, 1997).
5 Sir Robert Ensor, *England 1870–1914* (NY: Oxford University Press), p. 137.

women such as the great reformer, Hannah More – under the ministry of their Clapham Vicar, the Reverend John Venn, would all rise early to meet their Lord through Bible study and prayer.[6]

In both Britain and America we can recognise the general elevation of society following a Christian awakening. As the historian T.R. Glover has observed, 'Christianity stabilizes society without sterilizing it.' Morality, customs, idioms – and even language itself are affected. The phrase *'holding the fort'* – commonly used today – was a direct derivation from the hymn *'Hold the fort ...'* sung up and down England by Ira D. Sankey, D.L. Moody's soloist during his great campaigns in the late nineteenth century.

SYDNEY'S 'MR. ETERNITY'

Indeed, the testimony of a single convert can reach unimaginably far, into a nation's DNA. It was just after midnight in Australia when a brilliant galaxy of fireworks burst over Sydney's Harbour Bridge as the twentieth century bowed out on 31st December. As the glow subsided, eight gigantic letters, a hundred feet high, could be picked out in neon lights across the Bridge. They remained lit up throughout the night. They spelt out a single word: *'ETERNITY'*. This was Sydney's tribute to a man who had become a legend in the city's life, a former illiterate drunkard, Arthur Stace.

Earlier in the century, Arthur had wandered as a homeless down-and-out into St. Barnabas' Church, Broadway, and found himself faced by the question, *How and where are you going to spend Eternity?* The word 'Eternity' itself

6 Michael Hennell, *John Venn and the Clapham Sect* (UK: Lutterworth Press, 1958), p. 208.

became his one-word message to the entire city as – from then on – night after night he would chalk the word on sidewalks and walls in his newly acquired copperplate writing. This continued for twenty-five years – and no one knew who the anonymous artist was. It was only after his identity became disclosed that, from then on, he was known across Sydney as 'Mr. Eternity'. It is reckoned that he must have scripted his 'sermon' at least half a million times.

Four hallmarks of Revival ... but more can surely be submitted, in terms of the sharing of the faith by countless witnesses, and the consequent entry of literally hundreds of thousands of new believers into the Kingdom of God. And yet ... no one story of how the flame is lit in a person can ever match another.

'Then one of the elders asked me to give my address, adding, 'A short one, please, not longer than an hour.'[7]

---

7 René Monod, *Korean Revival* (UK: Hodder and Stoughton, 1971).

5

HOW THE FLAME IS LIT

'One loving spirit sets another on fire.'

St. Augustine (a.d. 354–430): *The City of God*

How do great spiritual awakenings begin? We must re-
iterate the remarkable fact that it is only as the central
figure of history – Jesus Christ – is introduced by personal witness, one to another, that the flame is lit. We have
only to turn to the New Testament book of Acts for this
to be established. The cyclonic expansion of the Christian
church along the sixty thousand miles of Roman roads
that embraced the Mediterranean began with a single in-
cident – the martyrdom of Stephen. Luke then writes of
the great persecution that broke out 'on that day,' and we
learn that *all except the apostles were scattered throughout Judea and Samaria.* Luke goes on to tell us that 'those
who had been scattered preached the word wherever they
went' (Acts 8:4).

And this is how it happens. 'The Gossiping of the
Gospel' – one-to-one – has always been the secret, from

that day to this. Let us never discount great stadium campaigns, for – even in these instances – *people will come because they were brought, and people will respond because they were prayed for!* However, we do not seem to find outstanding 'apostolic' preachers behind the astonishing spread of the Christian faith in China today.

THE CHINESE AWAKENING

Here is an awakening that may well turn out to be the greatest revival in all history. From all accounts, the emergence of new believers in China – numbering hundreds of thousands – has been happening in the absence of any organized campaigns or media hype. Sunday meetings are frequently held in a homestead, containing thirty or forty people – but with many others joining the occasion via social media. The church today in China is virtually uncontainable. Vitally, the whole process – as in the Acts of the Apostles – takes off on the wings of personal encounters.

Come to the New Testament, when the Greek evangelist Philip catches up with an Ethiopian on the way to Gaza (Acts 8:26-40). Is this how Africa itself was first reached? How had the Christian leader Timothy been previously reached, when the apostle Paul finally met him at Lystra? Had his believing grandmother been won, back at Pentecost?

Nearly always, it is 'one-to-one'. At the great Billy Graham 'Eurofest' Youth Event in Brussels, years ago, Harvey Thomas, the Director, put out a questionnaire to the eight thousand delegates from around Europe. One question read, 'How did you become a disciple of Christ?' Attendants were invited to itemize their answers from a list of possibilities – church meetings, family, big events and so forth. There was no mistaking the outstanding emphasis revealed by the returns. Easily top of the list was *the friendship of a Christian*. At the very bottom were *the receiving of a tract or pamphlet,* and *the witness of a stranger.*

True, there are indeed occasions when the one-off encounter brings a positive response. The evangelist John Chapman ('Chappo') of Sydney, Australia, once described stopping his car to give a lift to a hitch-hiker. He then opened conversation with the question 'And what do you do in life, mate?' It was natural, as they talked on, that the counter-question was put to John, 'And what do *you* do, then?' Chappo was ready with his response.

'The Church of England pays me to persuade people to become Christians.'

'How so?' came the bewildered reply. 'How do you set about persuading people?'

With the ground prepared, it was not too difficult for John to explain the way to entry into the Christian life … and the rest is history.

I was in the back of a car in Tanzania, when my African driver acted similarly for a man on the road. Conversation began in the Gogo dialect, with which I was unfamiliar. But then, as the car stopped by the roadside, I saw the two men bend their heads in prayer. When our passenger finally left us, I asked my driver what had been happening. He replied, 'That dear man has just received Christ into his life, and I was able to recommend a pastor who would help him onwards.'

'WE WISH YOU KNEW!'

Let us take up the story of a man born into a well-to-do Ugandan family, William Nagenda. He was a government clerk in the city of Entebbe when he first encountered for himself the Christian message. Seated at his desk one day, he heard the sound of joyful Gospel singing outside his office door. 'Tukutendereza Yesu' rang the song – 'We praise you Jesus.' Angrily he threw open the door.

'What's going on?' he demanded. 'What's this all about?'

Three smiling men were facing him. One of them was none other than the evangelist Simeoni Nsibambi.

'Ah,' they replied, 'we wish you knew!'

Enraged, William slammed the door in their faces. Then, sitting again at his desk, he began to reflect. *What is it about those three men – their faces? I've never seen faces quite like that ... so alive, so happy and fulfilled. I wish I could have a face like theirs!*

He came back to the three and put his query to them.

'Your faces!' he exclaimed. 'I would really like to have a face like yours – but what do I have to do for that to happen? What did you do to get faces like that?'

Their answer stunned him.

'Do?' they replied. 'Why – we have *done* nothing; nothing at all! If anything *has* changed in us' – and they pointed their fingers upwards – 'it is because of Him – our Saviour Jesus Christ. He has done it all!'

Riveted by their response, William returned to his desk, and by midnight he had turned in prayer and faith to Christ. A new evangelist had been born, whose voice would one day be heard across Africa, in Europe, Australia, America and around the world.

Jesus Christ became the complete focus of William's life. He would say to his friends, 'Don't let's always be talking about revival. Let's talk about Jesus.' Utterly self-effacing,

William was quiet, somewhat unfathomable – and at times uncomfortably discerning. Speaking to one of his protégés, I made the observation, 'I'm a little apprehensive of William. He has the ability to read my thoughts. Should I be unnerved?'

'No, not at all,' was the answer. 'It's true that William can tell if something is wrong in any of us – but it really doesn't matter, because if there is any confessing of sin to be done, it's always his own sins that he confesses first!'

William's preaching was to become in every way *alive* – in brilliantly African presentations, where stories, proverbs and incisive perceptions were intertwined with a Christ-centred winsome appeal and the boldest of challenges.

Preaching once in Weithaga's neighbouring township of Kahuhia I heard him as he spoke of Christ:

> Why, on the day of the Cross He could have had twelve legions of angels to look after Him! And there were those angels, ready up there in Heaven, looking down anxiously, as their Leader was being taken to die. 'Shall we go down now?' they were wondering. 'Is this the moment for us to scatter those soldiers, those priests, those people jeering at the Son of God? We will go down and stop all this, the moment we are given the word.' But no word came, and the angels were left, still looking down. They didn't know what to do!

Here was a sermon in true Nagenda style – preaching the message of the Cross, almost entirely from the viewpoint of the angels …

GRAVITY AND HUMILITY

Of no front-line evangelist was it ever said, 'He was a terribly funny man!' The tricks of oratory, one-line witticisms or plagiarism, are out. William exhibited – along with Richard Baxter, Charles Finney, George Whitefield and Billy Graham, both the gravity and humility that derives solely from one who sits at the feet of Christ.

One Sunday in England, I was speaking at an all-age gathering in St. Ebbe's Church, Oxford. My talk was illustrated with a home-made children's 'Visual Aid'! It was a jumble of cardboard, strings and sellotape. I was dumbfounded at the close to see William Nagenda – who had been sitting at the back – coming up the centre aisle towards me, his face aglow. 'Oh my!' he exclaimed. 'Praise God; that was for *me!*' I could barely stutter any meaningful reply.

But then, what of Festo Kivengere – who one day would preach at the graveside of William, his friend of a lifetime? Festo never knew his own age – 'I was born during Uganda's Rindepest cattle plague!' he would smile. His real 'beginning' he attributed to his spiritual new birth. It had begun when he and his best friend, Festo Rwamunahe, had laughingly been rebelling against the onset of Uganda's spiritual awakening.

'I was nearly caught that time!' panted Festo's companion. 'You should have seen them – you could hear the singing and crying a mile from the church. Then I ran for it. They'd have got me if I'd stayed!'

Festo Kivengere smiled. 'I warned you, didn't I? I told you that those meetings were terrible. You stick to me in the future – those people are mad!'

'GIVE ME ONE MORE WEEK!'

The change came one October Sunday – during much of which Festo had been drinking. But at six o'clock his fellow-rebel rode up on a bicycle, and his testimony came like a thunder-clap. 'When I was in church today, I accepted Jesus, and He has forgiven me of my sins.' Apologising for various wrongs he had committed, he rode off into the village.

Festo made for his room. 'I was kneeling, seeking forgiveness and restoration. I began to cry to God, and my eyes were opened to His love at the Cross. It seemed to me that the death of Christ was because of *me*. It was as if the Lord was saying, *'This is how much I love YOU.'* I felt a tremendous liberation. I jumped to my feet, singing and shouting alone in my room. I remember saying, 'Lord this is too much for me! Surely, I'm not likely to live long now! But give me permission for one more week! Just one more week – and I will tell everyone I meet about this!''

Festo rushed out of the room, and into the open air. A woman was passing by, a hundred yards away. 'Stop! Stop!' shouted Festo. 'Jesus has come my way!'

The woman tossed her head and turned away. Drunk … and on a Sunday! Undeterred, Festo ran on to the nearby church, where the members were coming out. The drums were still beating, and singing filled the air. Festo's sister and his niece were in the crowd. One look at his face and they rushed towards him. The whole group, electrified, escorted Festo back to his room, and the singing began again! No one went to bed that night; the joy was too great. The very next morning Festo was leading a geography lesson in Kigezi High School; but at once his pupils noticed the change. 'Sir, what has happened to you? How can we get what you have found?'

Festo later told me, 'When I finished telling them what had happened, some of them stood up to make their own commitment to Christ. No, I wasn't preaching – it was a geography lesson!'

Unlike William Nagenda, Festo had a bubbling out-going personality. He would not remain a school teacher for ever. Evangelism – and full-time ministry were to take over. One day he would become a bishop.[1]

Interpreting for Billy Graham in the mid-60s was a challenge for Festo. The only word in Swahili for 'sin' is the word *thambi*. There had to be found a way of avoiding such sequences as:

'They were guilty of *sin*!'
— 'They were guilty *of thambi*.'
'They had committed *iniquity*!'
— 'They had committed *thambi*.'
'The whole city was guilty of *unrighteousness*!'
'... er ... *thambi*'

Eventually the problem was solved when the American evangelist confidently advised, 'Don't bother to translate me literally. Just say what you know I mean!'

Two men, two lives – that were representative of a mighty army of those who have come under the magnetic spell of the Man of Galilee.

> *'Revive Thy work, O Lord!*
> *Exalt Thy precious name!*
> *And may Thy love in every heart*
> *Be kindled to a flame.'*

---

1 Anne Coomes, *Festo Kivengere: The Authorised Biography* (UK: Monarch Books, 1990).

6

'WAS IT A TRUE AWAKENING?'

*'Dear friends, do not believe every spirit, but test
the spirits to see whether they are from God.'*

(THE APOSTLE JOHN; 1 JOHN 4:1)

Professor Dallas Willard of California once wrote: 'Some
conservative and evangelical churches still sometimes talk
about *saving* the soul, but even this much less than used to
be the case; and once the soul is "safe" it is usually treated
as needing no further attention. *Ignoring the soul is one
reason why Christian churches have become fertile sourc-
es of recruits for cults and other religious and political
groups.*'[1]

I was once sitting among hundreds of others at a convention, held by an evangelical organization. The advertised topic for that morning, had been 'The Word of God
Today'. But upon starting, the speaker declared, 'The Lord
has told me to change the talk that had been announced
for today. Instead, I am going to give you my testimony.'

---

1 Dallas Willard, *Renovation of the Heart* (USA: NavPress, 2002), p. 208.

I remember thinking, '*You lazy thing; I've paid money to come here and hear you speak from the Bible*'. But that's what happens, when someone can't give the time to prepare for their accepted brief; they give their testimony!

And so it proved. Instead of 'The Word of God Today,' we were exposed to a cascade of egocentric experiences, sensational answers to prayer and stories of miraculous healings. As the talk continued, the speaker began to declare his diagnoses ... someone out there with cancer of the spine ... a woman suffering from severe rheumatism ... another with a disabled leg. Instant healing was claimed and confidently pronounced from the front.

While in full flow, however, the speaker was stopped by a tap on the shoulder – '*We must break – it's time for lunch!*' This proved no deterrent, however. 'No, no – there's still time for a few more miracles before lunch!'

But eventually we found ourselves in the dining room. Plates were being passed around. The previous hiatus seemed well and truly forgotten. We found ourselves murmuring politely, 'Pass the salt please ... would you like some sprouts?' Inwardly I thought, *In the face of a real miracle, we couldn't possibly be behaving like this; we would have been like Acts 3 – 'filled with wonder and amazement.'*

WHEN DISAPPOINTMENT RESULTS

It is not that we do not believe in prayer for healing! But disappointments can result when highly publicized events are held – under a visiting 'Personality' – with advertised promises of healings and miracles – to which the weak or disabled are brought in their wheelchairs. This has been lamentably true in Africa. As one who has been involved in the faithful work of *African Enterprise* (founded some decades ago by Michael Cassidy of South Africa), I have received critical observations from some of our loyal AE workers who had witnessed such meetings.

On one occasion the invitation had gone out from a travelling evangelist to infertile women in the city. They were encouraged to attend a rally with healings, and – as a sign of their faith – to bring a diaper *(nappy)* with them.

'Imagine the disillusionment that resulted,' commented one of our leaders. 'The evangelist having gone – and departed for another city – had left behind a trail of distress. We spent months afterwards trying to deal with the emotional aftermath experienced by so many distraught women.'

Furthermore, too often, in the life of the local church, I have had to counsel members who have attended a healing meeting led by an individual with no credentials whatever. In certain cases such practitioners have, self-confessedly, been mediums in the past. Apparent healings have even taken place, but the subsequent loss of peace or any awareness of Christ's sure presence would seem to indicate that the 'power' may indeed have come from an alien source – even from below; *it was never true healing.*

It would seem that the best environment for healing prayer is within the fellowship of the local church, where we know each other, where we may learn lessons from mistakes, and are well placed to follow up with ongoing care and prayerful support (James 5:14-18).

Although some spiritual movements may understandably be transitory in their lasting effect – such as the *Holy Rollers* of California's Azusa Street awakening of 1905 – the passage of time, nevertheless, provides us with a useful measure by which we can assess the degree to which any spiritual happening has truly drawn its power from 'The Spirit of truth' (John 16:13).

THE TEST OF TIME

It is not too difficult, for example, to learn from the now largely discredited 'Kansas City Prophets' who were making headlines in the late 1980s in Christian periodicals. Claims were being made that – by their uniquely inspired utterances – entire regions would be supernaturally transformed. Clairvoyant exposures of embarrassed sinners would be made in the crowds they addressed; and numerous dramatic prophecies were declared. It was the test of time, ultimately, that brought the group under concerned scrutiny – particularly when their bold and sometimes detailed prophecies yielded only partial fulfilment. They certainly fell short of the standard required by God's prophets of the Old Testament. Any prophet whose foretelling was not precisely fulfilled was declared a false prophet:

> 'They speak visions from their own minds, not from the mouth of the Lord.' (Jer. 23:16)

Supernatural out-of-body experiences were also claimed by some of the Kansas City leaders, in their accounts of having received divine confidences in the very throne room of heaven. The reputation of the prophets was further reduced by various inconsistencies of behaviour, including sexual misconduct. The movement had faded by the early 1990s.

Every true spiritual awakening will, despite many evident blessings, feature errors, mistakes and sins among its leaders – tainted as they inevitably are by the result of the human Fall. Only Time can give clarity in answering the question, 'Was it a true awakening?'

Even now we are a little too close fully to assess the 'Toronto Blessing' that began in 1994 at the Airport Vineyard Church in Toronto. Commonly termed 'The Latter Rain Movement,' it drew thousands of pilgrims from many parts of the world – inspired by reports of its message of love, fervent prayer, ecstatic overflowing joy and testimonies of personal burdens lifted and ailments healed. Newspapers and the Christian press were naturally quick to highlight the phenomena of holy laughter, mass collapses ('slaying in the spirit') and the testimonies of many that they had supernaturally received gold or silver fillings in their teeth during the meetings.

From Britain alone no less than twenty-five million pounds was spent on flights to Toronto, in the quest for spiritual blessing. Pam and I know many who attended and returned uplifted – testifying to an altogether new spiritual momentum in their souls.

Ultimately, time will tell as to the validity of any move-ment that comes to the public's attention – and so does the yardstick of the Bible.

Indeed, a Scripture applied by observers of any pow-erful movement will always raise the possibility of exag-geration and deviations – however minor – that suggest the unwelcome intervention of Satan, who 'will use all sorts of displays of power, through signs and wonders that serve the lie ...' (2 Thess. 2:9) Humble, then, are the leaders and participants in every awakening who carefully examine where the true centre lay. For while the external and initially supernatural manifestations of a revival will inevitably prove transitory, the true God-given centre – in Christ Himself – must surely endure.

Past history does provide us with powerful and painful lessons from movements whose foundations were not fully secured upon the Rock. A possible example lies in the controversial 'Irvingite' movement of the nineteenth century.

THE IRVINGITES

In my book on public speaking I have referred to the celebrated Scottish Presbyterian preacher, Edward Irving – instituted as Minister to a London church with a congregation of about fifty.[2] Within a year, hundreds were gathering to hear the flowing eloquence of London's latest sensation. The Sunday audiences included the English statesmen, George Canning and Robert Peel; the social reformers Jeremy Bentham and slave-trade abolitionist William Wilberforce; the poets Coleridge and Macaulay – and the future Prime Minister, William Gladstone. The current Prime Minister, Lord Liverpool, was among Irving's frequent hearers. People had to be admitted by ticket, and hundreds were turned away. *It was indeed hailed as a revival.*

But the crowds were being won by soaring oratory, rather than through the secure Biblical anchorage of the speaker. Eventually, it was the tediousness of the lengthy services that began to deter Irving's more intelligent admirers. As the gilt on the gingerbread began to wear thin, slowly the numbers dipped. In his attempt to win back his audience, Irving began to enter into the realms of what Dr. Andrew Drummond described as 'over-belief'.[3]

2 Richard Bewes, *Speaking in Public Effectively* (Tain: Christian Focus Publications, 2005).
3 Andrew Drummond, *Edward Irving and his Circle* (James Clarke & Co., Ltd, 1937).

The historian Thomas Carlisle (himself a friend of Irving) dryly observed, 'There was now the impossibility to live neglected, to walk on the quiet paths, where alone it is well with us. Singularity must henceforth succeed singularity.'

This trait of 'singularity' took Irving into the realms of millennialism, prophecy, the miraculous – and a craving for the Gifts of the Spirit. To ecstatic speech was eventually added automatic writing ... 'when sheets of paper would be covered with characters believed to be letters and words.'

Questions were even raised as to whether the prophecies of Mr. Irving should, word-for-word, be permanently preserved as God-inspired. Children, also, would be encouraged to prophesy. The Cornish diarist, Caroline Fox, gave her own account of a particular instance: *'The parents placed themselves entirely under the direction of these chits, who trotted about the house, and everything they touched was immediately to be destroyed or given away as Babylonish!'*

Irving identified every supernatural event as part of 'the latter days' – as representing his own time. The 'gifting' took many bewildering forms and indeed paralleled an earlier awakening in New England, with hundreds rolling on the ground, shrieking, jerking, braying like Balaam's donkey or 'barking on all fours'. By 1903 the 'holy laugh' and an over-free association of the sexes appeared. The New England excesses had led to two penetrating treatises by the eminent preacher Jonathan Edwards: *On the Religious Affections* and *On the Present Revival*. The first of Edwards' penetrating diagnoses was what he described as 'Undiscerned Spiritual Pride'.

Finally, Irving was deposed from his church over his increasingly unbalanced views on the nature of Christ, and he died in lonely disillusionment. The movement, that had looked so alive in the beginning, had ended like a burnt-out crater. His *Catholic Apostolic Church*, as it came to be called, would eventually continue from the ashes – characterized henceforth by a formalised sacramentalism.

Caution is needed today in the area where the Irvingites succumbed, for the Holy Spirit is a Person – never a 'movement'! Here too lay a failure to know the difference between the Prophetic and the Hysteric. It happens still that individuals can emerge from an event or conference, having apparently been Spirit-baptised, water-baptised, exorcised, 'filled' and healed – only to return to the one-room bed-sit, but days later finding themselves as confused or drained as some of Irving's adherents.

CHRIST'S SIX SAVING ACTIONS

History is not short of movements that have allowed themselves to slip – even fractionally at first – from the centrality of *Christ's six saving actions*. God's salvation in Jesus Christ was inaugurated by His birth at Bethlehem, achieved by His death at Calvary, affirmed by His resurrection at Easter, celebrated by His ascension at the mountain, personalised by His Spirit at Pentecost, and will be consummated at His final Return. *This is the bedrock* – and any departure from it can hijack an entire awakening, taking the vision off Christ and into even bizarre directions.

Festo Kivengere was once invited to a revival in South-East Asia, to help redirect the awakening from certain distortions. In one seminar that he was leading, a joyous Christian sprang up with his question: 'Listen! I have come to Jesus. I have been saved and born again! I have been filled with the Holy Spirit. I can speak in tongues – and I can work miracles! *Do I need Christ any more?'*

Festo told me later, 'I could see the abyss that had opened up! You could understand this dear man's logic; Step One was Christ, Step Two was the blessing of the Holy Spirit! So now – having moved on to Step Two, could he leave Step One behind? It took time to help him understand that, in the moment of receiving Christ, it is the Holy Spirit, who comes to indwell us – *to make the presence of Jesus real!'*

Men and women can be gripped by strange spiritual infections. For a few months or years even, they may revel in the new experiences, but after the fires of emotional extremes have died down, they are simply pumped out and empty. The result is either a lapse into total unbelief, or recourse to a different 'mother body' such as Roman Catholicism or Orthodoxy, in which they can feel both uninvolved and 'safe'.

REQUIRED CREDENTIALS

Unfortunate deviations such as the Irvingite experience need never happen, if there can only be a strong hand on the tiller. When, around A.D. 62 or 63, the Apostle Paul wrote to his trusted lieutenant Titus to 'straighten out' the confused church on the island of Crete, he reckoned on the reliability of this, his 'son in the faith' (Titus 1:4). There had been Cretans at Pentecost, and thus a church had become established on the island. But it was disordered and tough to handle. Crete was supposedly the birthplace of Zeus, and Bacchus was also worshipped. The church was young and shaky. But Titus had earned a good reputation during his previous journeys with Paul.

And what were the required credentials for this leader?
Why, ministers are to be 'blameless'. Blameless – *not flaw-
less!* Because leadership of God's people is a public office,
the requirement is for every church to examine the list of
qualities outlined in these 'pastoral' letters of Paul (see Titus 1:6-9 and 1 Tim. 3:1-7).

Titus was to hold to 'the trustworthy message, as taught by
the apostles' – in this single unswerving body of inspired belief. Paul's pastoral letters refer to *the teaching ... the faith ...
the truth ...* and *the deposit,* bequeathed to us. And there are
two sides to the ministry of God's Word to a church (v.9):

1. to 'encourage' and build up – that the sheep
   might be fed;
2. to 'refute' and correct – that the wolves might
   be dispatched!

Christian teaching was never a dead, fossilized thing. For
true gospel doctrine is the fuel that makes the fire burn.
Indeed, good theology and good ethics belong together.
The revealed, objective Word of the Lord our God has to
be our yardstick for ever!

The utter sadness of Edward Irving's 'Catholic Apostolic Church' – as it came to be called – is that its devotees
were never a credible advertisement for the teaching. In
the case of Titus, however, the slaves of Crete were to be
the model for others to learn from!

> 'Teach slaves to be subject to their masters in every-
> thing, to try to please them, not to talk back to
> them, and not to steal from them, but to show that
> they can be fully trusted, so that in every way they
> will make the teaching about God our Saviour at-
> tractive' (Titus 2:9-10).

That is to say, the slaves of Crete were to 'decorate' the Truth; to be seen as an attractive frame for the picture of Christ!

> 'Faithfully to teach the apostolic gospel of
> Christ will always prevent a childlike church
> from becoming a childish church.'

(DONALD ENGLISH AT THE KESWICK CONVENTION)

7

BACK TO THE CENTRE

*'Carry the Cross patiently, and with perfect
submission, and in the end it shall carry you.'*

(THOMAS À KEMPIS: *The Imitation of Christ*)

The hymn-books are a dead give-away! You've only to
pick up a copy of *Sacred Songs and Solos,* which – in the
time of the revival associated with Moody and Sankey –
sold no less than eighty million copies. A single glance
at the contents shows where the centre of the awakening
unmistakably lay. Whether the topics listed relate to The
Work of Christ, Salvation and the New Birth, Forgiveness,
Assurance, Holiness and Surrender, Evangelism and The
Missionary Call ... or simply 'Gospel Songs' – we are
never far from the power of the Blood at Calvary.

Indeed, if we were asked to define the make-up of the
Christian faith, it can be done with a single word from
the Greek New Testament. It is the word *hapax* – 'once
for all'. In the book of Jude, verse 3, we are exhorted to
contend for the faith that was *'once for all'* entrusted to the

saints. Couple that with Hebrews 7:27 and we learn that Christ was sacrificed for our sins *'once for all'* – it is the same word. What God has *said* then, He has said 'once for all' … we may not add to His Word by a single iota. Further, what God has *done*, He has done 'once for all'. There can be no 'Plus' tagged on to the message of the Cross. Across the centuries, the shadow of the Cross has straddled the world of religion, philosophy and politics – as the old hymn puts it – 'towering o'er the wrecks of time'.

The message has been relentlessly attacked through the years – including by those of the church who should know better. They will ask, 'Why did Jesus see Himself as a *sacrifice* for sins, by the shedding of blood?' But there it is – in the letter to the Hebrews and chapter 9 … a repeated emphasis on *'the blood'* of Christ … in verses 12, 14, 18, 19, 20 and 21; and then the summary in verse 22: 'Without the shedding of blood there is no forgiveness.'

GOD'S PROTOTYPE

Such passages – with their numerous allusions to priests, sacrifices, the Tabernacle and the Most Holy Place – give us one obvious reason why we cannot ignore the Old Testament, and books such as Leviticus. For there we are given God's prototype, His model for the way to forgiveness and the life of holy living. Even when the Israelites under Moses were making these animal sacrifices for sin, it was not they who were offering them! These were *the Lord's provision* for His people's forgiveness, as an education for them in advance of the Cross of Calvary itself.

Twenty-first-century readers might complain, 'But how repelling; all this about the sacrifices and burnt offerings and the altar – and this Jewish crudity about sprinkling the blood … as somehow pleasing to God?'

'Very primitive,' nod the connoisseurs. 'Give us the classics any day; the ancient Greeks or the Romans, and their outstanding civilizations.'

But those same connoisseurs too often choose to forget the blood, the human blood, that flowed from the altars and ritual celebrations of those heathen kingdoms. The city of Athens had a man and a woman sacrificed every year in the festival dedicated to the Delian Apollo. In another era, the Aztecs sacrificed hundreds of people every year, to maintain a relationship with their gods.

By contrast, human sacrifice was no part of God's true revelation – not until His own *self*-sacrifice, uniquely given in the blood of the Cross of Golgotha, at the central point of the world's redemption. And 'blood' meant death. Blood – when it is separated from the body – no longer signifies life; it means death – and a violent death at that.

THE PASSION OF CHRIST

After the showing of the film *The Passion of Christ*, a contact at my tennis club began an email correspondence with me. He had asked, 'If Jesus was to die for the sins of the world, why couldn't He just die quietly in bed?'

No one had ever asked me that question before.

I replied, 'The death of the crucifixion – attended and applauded even by the respected religious leaders – demonstrates the all-time depths of human wickedness; which, when presented with the purest Being who ever walked the earth, could only yell, 'Let Him be crucified!' – and then laugh and jeer as they watch the victim slowly die.

'That was part of it.' I added, 'The Cross says for ever, *that's how ugly your sin is.*

'But,' I continued, 'it also demonstrates for us *how high the love of God is* – in reaching down to a bunch of rebels, to save them from the loneliness of self-inflicted outer darkness. In the Cross our eternal loneliness was to be endured by Himself, in the Person of his Son, so making the offer of forgiveness full and free to all. There's nothing like the blood of Christ to humble us and turn our hearts.'

From early days, God's ancient people needed this education themselves! Those *prototype* animal sacrifices – offered centuries before the Crucifixion – acted a little like the temporary 'cover note' that insurers will offer on a car owner's damaged car... . until the document proper arrives. The Cross – the shadow of which falls both forwards and backwards upon the highroads of time – is our document proper.

Some might say, 'I don't like to think of an animal having its blood shed so that others can go free.' Good. *We should tremble* that the blood of another is to be acceptable on our behalf. Yet this was all part of the centuries-long build-up of our Gospel education.

Come to the day of the Crucifixion outside Jerusalem. And there, hanging between two criminals is the Substitute-Saviour – His blood shed, once and for all. Later the Apostle Paul referred to the Church of God – 'which,' he wrote, 'He (God) *bought with His own blood*' (Acts 20:28). Here is the only sentence in Scripture that declares that it was the blood of God Almighty that was shed at Calvary – thereby Himself intercepting His own judgment upon humanity.

It was the very understanding of 'Sacrifice' that helped to inspire the Revival in East Africa. 'We knew all about sacrifice,' smiled Bishop Festo Kivengere. 'Even in my early days as a little herd-boy, we were making tiny sacrifices to the gods – though, in our hearts, we knew that they were pitiful offerings! So when the message of the Cross finally arrived, it made perfect sense. We knew there *had* to be something better.'

WHEN A SHUDDER RAN THROUGH NATURE

The wrath of divine judgment isolated the Son of God, that day outside Jerusalem – as the loneliest person in the Universe. 'Look at Him!' was the verdict. 'There's the cheat; there's the liar, there's the deceiver, adulterer, fraudster, paedophile' ... *and then the scene is blotted out.* The sky goes dark, the earth rumbles, the Temple curtain tears apart. As the Christian Jew, Alfred Edersheim, once wrote, 'A shudder ran through nature.' In the blackness of it all, is uttered that cry from Psalm 22, which perfectly expresses the desolation of an innocent sufferer: 'My God, my God, why hast thou forsaken me?'

The blood of God's New Covenant was being shed in fulfilment of the gift, prophesied in Jeremiah 31:34 – and quoted in the letter to the Hebrews: 'For I will forgive their wickedness, and their sins I will remember no more.'

Even the forgiven sinner may be found praying, 'Lord, am I really forgiven for that terrible thing I did those years ago? I can't bear to think of it. *You must hate me.*' But then comes the divine reply, 'What thing? I don't remember it.' Those sins will never confront us again at the Judgment. This is a mighty miracle; God possesses the capacity to 'forget' the sins of His repentant people. The file on us is empty.

Calvary, then, is Judgment Day *in advance*. Incredibly, our sin has already been judged! Theologians call this stupendous truth 'penal substitution'. It is all to do with the penalty, the judgment – deserved by us – but borne by the Lord God Himself in the Person of His Son. There are different important facets of the Cross, but the principle of substitution – basic to our belief, from the book of Leviticus onwards – is the core and reality behind them all.

A BREAKFAST WITH JOHN STOTT

I was once having breakfast with my longstanding mentor and neighbour, John Stott, and a few other friends. It was then that John – in a simple five-minute 'thought' – gave us some vital theological terms relating to the Cross – behind all four of which stands the principle of Substitution.

'First,' he said, 'the Blood means *Penalty Paid*. Here, the theological word is *redemption* – the language of the slave market. A price has been paid, and it was 'the precious Blood of Christ' (1 Pet. 1:18-19).

'Secondly,' said John, 'the Blood means *Wrath Averted*, the theological word being *propitiation* – this word being the best translation of Romans 3:25 or 1 John 2:2 ('He is the propitiation for our sins').' 'This,' continued John, 'is the language of the Tabernacle; and of the Temple. It's a powerful word, because it doesn't have "sin" as its object. You don't propitiate sin! It is God Himself who needs to be propitiated; his holy wrath appeased, set aside and averted – if we are not to remain an offence to Him.'

The coffee was now cold. John went on: 'The fact that God was to be propitiated demonstrates that the shed blood of Christ actually *did* something to God Himself. This is why the old King James Version was correct (as

is the English Standard Version of today) in its use of the
word *propitiation* – against the weaker phrase of some
modern versions, *a sacrifice of atonement*.

'But the Blood also means *Righteousness Exchanged,*'
added John. 'Here, the Bible word is *justification* ... and
it's the language of the Law Courts. How – despite my
sin – can I be treated as though I had never transgressed?
It could only be accomplished by Christ, standing in my
place, so that His righteousness could be credited to *me,*
while my sin and its due reward was attributed to *Him*.
The very word *Justification* has no parallel in any other
belief system.'

We stayed, riveted, around the breakfast table.
'Then, finally,' said John, 'the Blood means *Relationship
Restored,* and the word there is *reconciliation*; and here
is the language of the Family. It's there in Romans 5:9-11,
and it's there in Jesus' story of the Prodigal Son in
Luke 15. We have it in the statement of God in Christ,
"reconciling the world to himself," this happening at the
Cross where – as our Substitute *"He was made sin for
us"'* (2 Cor. 5:18-21).

'Here,' said John, 'are four wonderful effects of the
Cross in the life of a believer, and the rock principle behind every one of them is penal substitution – *Christ instead of me*, "for even the Son of Man did not come to be
served, but to serve, and to give his life as a ransom for
(Greek: instead of) many" – Mark 10:45.'

Our party broke up. 'Thank you, John,' said one sen-
ior colleague, 'I've learnt something!'

'What about preaching this for us at All Souls,
John?' I asked. 'I can see it coming up, maybe in four
future sermons! And then maybe ... a book?' And so it

happened – finally resulting in a major book that has gone across the world, *The Cross of Christ* (Inter-Varsity Press).

THE PRINCIPLE MAKES SENSE

Sixteen centuries ago John Chrysostom of Constantinople had expressed the 'penal substitution' principle when he declared: 'God was about to punish them; this He did not do. They were about to perish; but He gave His only Son *instead of them.*'

The Substitution principle ... it can make sense, even to young children, who – when asked by their mums, 'Will you go shopping "for" me?' – know exactly what is meant. They are saving their mother from the task. If they go shopping, *she need not;* they are doing it "for her". That is precisely the principle behind the phrase 'Jesus died for me.'

We must try to understand those who question what happened at the Cross – in withering terms of 'Cosmic Child Abuse'. Like us, perhaps, they have found it hard to take in the wonderful and enduring truth of the Trinity – at work for our salvation! This was a Salvation:

Authorized by the Father in heaven
Achieved by the Son on the Cross
Activated by the indwelling Spirit in the heart.

There are those who take exception to the Bible word 'wrath'. There are hymn book publications and churches that refuse to feature the well-known Townend/Getty hymn 'In Christ Alone' on account of the two lines which read: 'Till on that cross as Jesus died, The wrath of God was satisfied' ...

But our Reformers had it right – in the Church of England Prayer Book – where, at the heart of the Communion

Service, this truth described Christ's death on the Cross ...
'who made there, by his one oblation of himself once offered, a full, perfect, and sufficient sacrifice, oblation, and
satisfaction, for the sins of the whole world.'

Let us repeat: although the Cross presents us with the
profoundest event in history, you do not need a Ph.D. to
take it in; its message is as simple for worshippers of the
Lord in a Masai dwelling on Kenya's Ngong Hills as it is
for a C.S. Lewis or an Aleksandr Solzhenitsyn. A twelve-
year-old boy, after hearing a message on The Cross, wrote
a letter:

'Dear Sir, yesterday evening I gave my heart to Jesus,
and this morning I feel as if tons and tons of lead had been
lifted off my heart.'

> *'Oh, make me understand it,*
> *Help me to take it in,*
> *What it meant to Thee, the Holy One,*
> *To bear away my sin.'*

8

RUIN AND REVIVAL

*'When the storm passes over,
the grass will stand up again.'*

(Kikuyu proverb from East Africa)

It had indeed been a stormy and dark period during the two hundred largely leaderless days of the Judges, there in Israel, in what must have been part of the Bronze Age. Then a little boy was born in answer to the impassioned prayer of a godly woman, Hannah, in the hill country (1 Samuel chapters 1 and 2) – and an altogether brighter new era for God's people was about to dawn. A revival it was indeed going to be – and none too soon.

In gratitude, Hannah's child, Samuel, was dedicated for the service of God; in fact he would live in the house of God at Shiloh. This temple had replaced Israel's former 'tent of meeting' (the Tabernacle), and it housed there the Ark of the Covenant in which were placed Moses' tablets of stone. Every year Hannah would make 'a little robe' for her boy, Samuel, as he went about his duties as a young trainee, assisting Eli, the priest at Shiloh's temple. The Jewish historian Josephus tells us that Samuel was only twelve years old at the time.

'In those days the word of the Lord was rare; there were not many visions' (1 Sam. 3:1). We can see the young Samuel curled up in a little ball, close to 'the lamp of God' that was still alight – when he hears a Voice calling him by name. We learn from the Scriptures that 'Samuel did not yet know the Lord.'

He gets up and runs to Eli.

'You called me!'

'Not me, sonny,' comes the reply, 'you go back and lie down.'

It happens again: *'Samuel ... Samuel ...'*

Again, he runs to Eli's bedside but is sent back: 'No, it's not *me* calling. Get back to bed!'

It happens a third time – and now realization dawns upon Eli, who then tells his young assistant:

'Next time just reply, "Speak, Lord, for your servant is listening."'

Samuel does so – and receives his divine commission that very night. He had gone to sleep as a boy probationer, but – by the time the sun rose next morning, as he got up to open the doors of the house of God – he was a prophet, about whom, years later, it would be said, 'When Samuel spoke, all Israel listened.'

'THERE WERE NOT MANY VISIONS'

Evidently the message that Samuel was commissioned to declare to his people would 'make the ears of everyone who hears of it tingle ...' (1 Sam. 3:11) – and there, perhaps, lies the key sentence of this remarkable account.

For a long, long time no one's ears had 'tingled' at all in Israel!

It was now around 1050 B.C. – and the story of the church of that time was characterised by a demoralized priesthood, an alienated people, and a silent God.

Then it was that the child Samuel came into the story of Israel, to close off the unprincipled era of the Judges – when authority in the land was at its lowest ebb and people lived according to their own standards of morality. The great exploits of Moses and Joshua were buried in the dust-laden archives of the past. As far as the word of the Lord was concerned, there seemed to be a famine in the land, and spirits were starving. *The Tabernacle* – the travelling portable worship tent of Moses' wilderness days – was no more than a static institution at Shiloh's temple. Eli himself was a spent force. The ministry of the priesthood was in general contempt, and the observation that 'there were not many visions' was a marvellous understatement.

A new expectation had been sparked into being that significant night in Shiloh, with the Ark of the Covenant still under guard, and the lamp of God still alight.

A TINGLING REVELATION

Wonderful revivals have occurred in the wake of even the darkest days, and have so often characterised the history of God's church. Revival rarely begins during times of material prosperity. Ruin and Revival seem to walk hand in hand, as in the time of America's Third Great Awakening in the 1850s, when financial crises, massive unemployment, superstition and crime were on the march. There have been decades – even centuries – when the world seemed to be in a long sleep. Then a scholar called Wycliffe would come alive to the message of the Bible; a Reformer like Luther would begin to shake all of Europe, and martyrs like Cranmer, Ridley and Latimer would light 'a fire which will never go out'.

We might have argued that surely *Eli* was the one to whom God's word should have come – at an era when Israel had lost its poetry, its very soul. Surely we would look for some experienced Sage to touch the world once more? But here, the story of Samuel's call appeals to us because it fits in with all that Jesus was to teach nearly eleven centuries later ... that you can only *perceive, understand* and *grasp* the rule and kingdom of God if you have the outlook of a child. The Scottish preacher of the nineteenth century, George Matheson, declared that, however grown up we are, 'It is by the survival of our childhood that we see the kingdom of God.'

Lose that – and we become cynical, hard and unbelieving; we cease to wonder and to give thanks, and fail even to recognise God's awakening when it comes.

God chose to pick a twelve-year-old – and suddenly the Bible started to grow again! Centuries earlier, there had been long periods when everything had come to a halt. Between Joseph's arrival in Egypt, and the call of Moses there were four hundred years! What were the people of God doing out there, in the alien surroundings of Egypt?

And then one day, God preserves the life of a little Hebrew boy, floating in the bulrushes of the river Nile – and builds him into a prophet and a leader who would take the Hebrews on the long trek that would lead them to their promised land. Here, it was the same in the case of Samuel, the long soulless 300-year stretch of the Judges was about to end, with the call to a boy sleeping by the lamp of God.

It would be the same after the prophet Malachi, at the close of the Old Testament. Four hundred long years would elapse before the Child of Destiny was born in remote Bethlehem. God's revelation would take a mighty dispensational leap forward – and the world would never be the same again.

Eventually the monotonous era of the judges had to pass, when corruption and compromise would finally be exposed. Eli, though seemingly godly and devout, had let Shiloh's temple slide into general contempt. His two sons, Hophni and Phinehas, were running the worship – and they were a couple of self-serving wheelers and dealers. They had abused their privileges as priests of the Lord. They grabbed more than their share of the sacrifices, and frequently by force. Worse still; Israel's central place of worship was being used for immoral purposes. Eli knew what was happening, but seemed unable to do more than issue his sons with a mild rebuke.

The light of Eli and his family was to go out, when his sons were both killed by the Philistines. At the news that the precious Ark itself had been captured, Eli, in shock, fell and broke his neck.

It has always been the challenge facing the church: Where is the yardstick of truth and purity? The penalty of faithlessness is public disarray and Christ's removal of the lamp of God from our lampstand (Rev. 2:5).

In the rejuvenation of Israel that took place, Samuel was not a founding prophet, like Moses, nor was he exactly a reforming prophet, like Elijah. He was more of a *preserving prophet* – in helping Israel to find her soul again. Under the ministry of Samuel, the people were able to say, 'We've found ourselves again; God is among us, and He's speaking.'

In our own era, we have a number of modern stories that tell of how a great gospel renaissance can take place – well below the radar of the internet and the public media; invisible – except to God. We can take the Diocese of Bor in the Southern Sudan as a riveting example.

A TINGLING ILLUSTRATION

I can never forget a Christian meeting in London, during which I interviewed one of the most influential and dedicated bishops that South Sudan has ever known; his name – Nathaniel Garang. Having been made a bishop in the Anglican tradition, his diocese consisted initially of four parishes. He came into leadership at the height of what was called The Bush War, in which villages were ravaged, and hundreds were being killed in the crossfire. Then, to great consternation, Nathaniel Garang disappeared from view. It was thought that he must have been killed in the wartime skirmishing. For five long years nothing further was known of him; nor indeed of anything that was happening in his diocese; no successor was appointed to his position.

But at long last the bishop emerged to civilized society again, thinner and greyer – but with an account of the Gospel's power that seemed to re-enact the Acts of the Apostles. Ignited by a contagious love of Christ, he had set about visiting and developing his diocese with no car, van, bicycle or any other modern resources, as he trudged his way on foot from village to village through the bush.

During the interview I asked him, 'No transport at all then, Bishop?'

'No, none,' he replied. 'Any car – or bicycle – would have been stolen very quickly. The war had seen to that.'

'So how did you get from village to village?' I asked.

'I would walk,' came the answer. 'I would walk all day, and then when I got to the next destination I would preach, evangelise, baptize – and pray with the people. We would continue this way through the night.'

'So you'd walk all day, and pray and preach all night?' I went on. 'You must have become very tired.'

'No … I never get tired,' replied the Bishop.

A MODERN JABEZ

It indeed emerged that, during those five years of South Sudan's ruin, the 'missing' Bishop had, by his untiring efforts, enlarged his diocese from its four parishes to over two hundred and fifty – and each with hundreds upon hundreds of new Christian disciples. Today South Sudan has no less than thirty entire Anglican dioceses. Here in Nathaniel Garang was a modern Jabez whose borders were *'blessed and enlarged'* by God (1 Chron. 4:9-10).

And to continue; it was during the height of the continuing troubles in the Sudan that the then Archbishop of Canterbury felt motivated to pay a visit to the troubled region. I was later to learn from his travelling colleague, Ian Smith, of the astounding reception that they received. Flying in from Kenya in a small propeller-driven aeroplane, they were able to evade dangers from the north as they made their landing in Sudan's southern region. In Ian's words:

> As the pilot switched off the engine, we were dumbfounded to hear the sound of tremendous drumming and shouting from not too far away! Then – over the hilltop – in they came – hordes of

shrill yelling Sudanese, brandishing what looked like spears in their hands as they charged towards us. My heart turned over with trepidation. Had we landed in the wrong place? But all was well; within seconds we realized that these were not only Christians, but many of them turned out to be members of the Sudanese Mothers' Union! The 'spears' were none other than wooden crosses, carefully decorated with empty shells and shrapnel from the war.

In seconds, our little aeroplane – and we ourselves – were engulfed with peals of singing in a pageant of joy and shouts of 'Hallelujah' all around us. We were then required to embark on a further journey to our next destination – in a spirit of gospel carnival. It was one of the most electrifying moments of my life.

And so it has been, that South Sudan – which has never been without bloodshed, poverty and utter ruin – has nevertheless been one of the fastest-growing churches in the world.

True; even against the darkest backdrop, the humble servant of God – whether a leathery veteran bishop or a young church trainee – may echo words by J.D. Burns:

> *'Oh, give me Samuel's ear!*
> *The open ear O Lord,*
> *Alive and quick to hear*
> *Each whisper of Thy word;*
> *Like him to answer at Thy call,*
> *And to obey Thee first of all.'*

9

WHEN THE SPIRIT MOVES

*'What if the full power of the Holy Spirit were to
be loosed today through all true believers? The
world could again be turned upside down.'*

(Billy Graham)

Taking the Reverend Erica Sabiti on his first tour of London was an unforgettable experience for me. 'Erica' was a Ugandan pastor, fired by the Revival that was touching the country area of his African home, and I was little more than a student, living in London. I knew only a little of the pastor's history. I did not know that in his earlier days Erica – with his 'Revival' connections – had been turned down for any church post by the authorities, as being 'unfit for any position of responsibility.' Little did I know, as we boarded the bus into London, that I had in my charge the future Archbishop of Uganda. God has a sense of humour!

Our first major stop-off was at the world-famous waxworks of Madame Tussaud's in Marylebone Road. To begin with, Erica simply couldn't take it in: that the colourful figures facing him from the world of history, sport, entertainment – and even royalty – were all of wax – and therefore lifeless. 'I feel I could touch him!' whispered my companion as we passed Winston Churchill. He was a little taken aback, however, when one of the figures before him *moved*, proving however only to be the smiling attendant at the exit.

MOVING STAIRS

The next challenge was the novelty of the London Underground! This caused my Ugandan charge considerable apprehension as we faced what to him was a set of 'moving stairs'. I kept close, as – tentatively – Erica put one foot forward. Naturally the escalator didn't wait for the other foot! But with my gentle pressure on his back he managed, and by the time we reached the top he was smiling with relief.

My task that day had simply been that of a guide who knew his way around London. It was years later when, on meeting Erica Sabiti as a revered and honoured leader in an international church setting, I could only inwardly feel that speaking to him was like speaking with Jesus. Here, I thought, is a man truly filled with the very Spirit of God. I, who had once encouraged him up the moving stairs of the London Underground, was now being escorted up a very different kind of Escalator altogether.

The wonderful fact about meeting someone who reminds us of Christ is that it is indeed Christ's unseen 'Other Self' who has come to live in that individual in the person of the promised Holy Spirit (John 14:18).

And this is the wonder of Pentecost. There is mutual recognition of one another when Christians meet from around the world; we see something of Christ in each other's eyes, in speech, in every mannerism. When the Holy Spirit is at work, it is unmistakable – *life in the Spirit of Christ is caught as much as taught.* This had all been part of Joe Church's original quest for what he had called 'The Highest', when suffering from failure and disappointment in his earlier days as a medical missionary. The power of the Holy Spirit changed everything.

REVIVAL REQUIRES DEFLATION

Yet the coming of revival involves Christ's followers in a costly love. For here, in Him is 'A Fellowship of the Deflated'! For one of the greatest men who ever lived – Paul of Tarsus – his whole experience of confrontation with Christ in the power of the Spirit blinded his natural pride. Until his journey to Damascus for the arrest of the hated Christians, his ideas, his training and his theology of impeccable Pharisaism were supposedly 'big' enough to make others bow to his authority. Until his conversion, Paul was something like a balloon at bursting point. But Saul could only become *Paul* when he was 'deflated' to nothing, in the very presence of the glorified Son of God, in his abject cry, 'Who are you, Lord?' (Acts 9:1-9).

In future days he would be ignominiously let down from the walls of Damascus in a basket, to escape arrest. He would be hounded across the seas by his enemies. He would be beaten until thought dead. He would be kept in prison without his books, lonely, cold and bored. Yet here was a man filled with the Spirit in his promotion across Europe of the message of Christ crucified.

Among the great 'killers' of spiritual life in the church of God are Gossip, Jealousy, Pride and Grumbling.

These sins – together with others – are all too frequently expressed today by email. Reputations have been demolished and whole ministries derailed by the insinuous use of a multiple email – a favourite tactical device of the Devil. We may hesitate over the inclusion of 'grumbling' in this unseemly list – but the apostle Paul includes it along with idolatry in his listing of Israel's sins in the wilderness (1 Cor. 10:6-10). No revival can take hold of a community when these evils are accommodated within the Church – from bishops through to the pastors; to church staff, group leaders, council members and right on to the grave diggers …

WHEN JEALOUSY TAKES OVER

William Sangster told the old fable of how the Devil was once crossing the Libyan desert, and came upon a group of junior devils who were tempting a holy hermit. They tried him with immoral seductions; they put doubts before his mind, and told him that his disciplined living was a waste of time. All proved useless – the holy man stayed holy!

Then the Devil stepped in. He said to the demons, 'Your methods are so crude, so ham-fisted! Permit me … !'

Then going up to the hermit he said, 'Have you heard the news? Your brother has been made Bishop of Alexandria.' It was only then that the face of the holy man began to twist and contort with jealousy and hurt pride.

None of us, but none of us, are immune!

In a revival fellowship open-air meeting at my old Kenyan homestead of Weithaga, I have seen a man – while giving his testimony of blessing in Christ – being ruthlessly pulled down in mid-sentence by those surrounding him – 'for hypocrisy'.

'Vainglory' is the King James' Version of the word for 'conceit' in Galatians 5:26 – and the Greek word there accurately depicts the 'puffed-up-balloon' concept – used in the New Testament of 'Diotrephes, who loves to be first' (3 John 9). It identifies an outlook described once by that late convert to Christ – the journalist Malcolm Muggeridge – as *'the dark little dungeon of my own ego'*.

Once allow the reviving Spirit of the Lord to inspire and preside – and several distinguishing features should characterize the true Gospel church. First:

THE SPIRIT-FILLED CHURCH IS MORE AWARE OF CHRIST THAN IT IS OF THE SPIRIT

There is this strange anonymity about the Holy Spirit. He is not given to us primarily to draw attention to Himself, but to Christ. As the Lord predicted of the Spirit, 'He will bring glory to me, by taking from what is mine and making it known to you' (John 16:14). I have sometimes been asked by Christian friends, 'Is yours a Holy Spirit church?' The answer must be that the hallmark of a genuine 'Holy Spirit' church is that it is unmistakably centred in Jesus Christ.

The same must apply to the individual. At the height of the East African Revival, Festo Kivengere was asked one day, 'Are you filled with the Holy Spirit?'

Festo replied, 'Well – you've been listening to me for the last forty minutes; what do *you* think?' Festo was being very 'New Testament'! For nowhere in the Acts of the Apostles did any individual publicly claim to be filled with the Holy Spirit. It was the *observers* of Stephen the martyr, for example, who recognised that he was filled with the Spirit. The best answer, then, to the question, 'Are you filled with the Spirit?' is, 'You'd better ask my wife! ... my husband! ... Ask my Boss – they'll tell you!'

There were two great gifts offered to the apostle Peter's hearers on the Day of Pentecost. They were Christ's 'forgiveness of your sins' and 'the gift of the Holy Spirit'. Following repentance, both gifts would immediately follow. This was an offer – universally made – to the hearers and their families, to alien peoples; indeed to 'all whom the Lord our God will call' (Acts 2:38, 39). *Here was a salvation offer, open for anyone in the world to accept.*

Forgiveness was the gift to bring cleansing to the soul. The Holy Spirit was the gift to bring power to the life! From Day One, the new believer is assured of New Birth by the Spirit, the 'anointing' of the Spirit, the 'sealing' of the Spirit and the 'Baptism' of the Spirit. The tenses of the Greek New Testament teach us this; that – for the new believer, every one of these blessings has already been bestowed! This is thrillingly spelt out in Billy Graham's *The Holy Spirit* (Thomas Nelson, 1978). It remains for the Christian, then, *to develop further* this life in the Spirit, to 'walk,' to 'pray', to 'fight' with the Spirit's help. And – as a way of life – we may daily pray to be 'filled' with the Spirit; or – as the Greek text has it, to 'go on being filled with the Holy Spirit' (Eph. 5:18).

Remarkably, the necessary qualification for even the *administrators* in the early church was that they should be selected on the basis that they were 'known to be full of the Spirit and wisdom' (Acts 6:3). Could we ever foresee this qualification being announced as a *requirement* in a local church's appointment of, say, the church's treasurer, stewards, PA team, caterers, or council members? Indeed, would we actually be happy to know that any such officer was *not* filled with the Spirit?!

Even in the car, as we drive to church on Sunday, Pam and I pray for this 'filling' – for ourselves and all involved at church, that – like the exiled John on the Island of Patmos we may all be 'in the Spirit on the Lord's Day!' (Rev. 1:10).

But here is a further distinguishing mark of Revival:

THE SPIRIT-FILLED CHRISTIAN IS MORE CONCERNED WITH INWARD CHARACTER THAN OUTWARD SHOW

This had been the Apostle Paul's concern about the Spirit-filled claims of his friends at Corinth. They were fascinated with the whole realm of supernatural manifestations – but to the exclusion of their moral standards. 'Brothers,' wrote Paul, 'I could not address you as spiritual but as worldly – mere infants in Christ …' (1 Cor. 3:1). He goes on to lament the worldliness of their jealousy, quarrelling and sexual immorality. Naturally, an obvious rejoinder to any claim of supernatural blessing is that asked directly by my late saintly aunt, Carol Hunt. On receiving such a testimony from a Christian friend, she exclaimed, 'How lovely! Now – *has it made you a nicer person!'*

'Remove the blockages to blessing!' is the vital call when 'revival' is in the air. It requires a ruthless attitude to personal sin – expressed in personal repentance and cleansing. Martin Luther likened the process to a river in spate in his quoted words: 'You cannot clean out the stable with barrows and shovels. Turn the Elbe into it!'[1]

Here too is a third revival characteristic:

---

1 J.S. Exell, *The Biblical Illustrator: 2 Timothy* (London: James Nisbet & Co), p. 112.

THE SPIRIT-FILLED PERSON IS MORE CONCERNED WITH 'EMPTYING' THAN WITH 'FILLING'

This is the wonder of the Spirit's working in the great democracy of the Gospel — when the spiritual tide is in. Those caught up in the flow will be concerned to promote the interests of others in the fellowship, rather than their own. Here is the principle of self-emptying in the service of Christ. When they are given something to do, their prayer will not be 'I am waiting for You to fill me before I can do it.' Rather they find to their joy that, in the obedient doing of God's will, fullness and 'filling' take place! The principle is:

> *Obeying, not 'waiting'*
> *Sharing, not 'hoarding'*

And that, seemingly, is how a man or woman is filled with the Holy Spirit for service. The filling of the Spirit is a necessarily ongoing experience. We are to remove the blockages, obey the Lord and share our blessings. To our amazement, when the task is done, we are likely to feel satisfied, fulfilled – even exhilarated – and certainly 'closer' than before we embarked upon it.

Be amazed! Paradoxically, *the way to be filled is to be emptied.*

How far are these qualities of a revived people exhibited in our own local fellowships?

'Therefore, as God's chosen people, holy and dearly loved, clothe yourselves with compassion, kindness, humility, gentleness and patience. Bear with each other and forgive whatever grievances you may have against one another. Forgive as the Lord forgave you. And over all these virtues put on love, which binds them all together in perfect unity' (Col. 3:12-14).

Jude – the earthly half-brother of Jesus – warned his readers against discipleship dictated by those who followed 'the way of Cain, ... shepherds who feed only themselves, clouds without rain, blown along by the wind ... autumn trees without fruit and uprooted – twice dead ... wild waves of the sea, foaming up their shame ... wandering stars, for whom blackest darkness has been reserved for ever' (Jude vv. 11-13).

SHOOTING STARS

The church today has sometimes been disastrously led by populist careerists. But Paul, Peter, John and Jude had – in their own time – faced these 'shooting stars' themselves. Always there have been practitioners who use every opportunity and every circle of influence in their concealed quest for self-advancement. They can never accept criticism. Their names may get widely trumpeted as they rise triumphantly into the ecclesiastical firmament — accompanied by cries of admiration. Yet, how could such masquerade ever prove durable in the eternal mission of God?

Wherever the Spirit moves, *grace* will always be apparent, for 'the servant of the Lord must not strive' (2 Tim. 2:24 KJV). And although there will always be joy in the soul, there will also be the *gravitas* that takes account of the Spirit's conviction of sin, righteousness and judgment — for no enquirer ever came to the foot of Calvary's Cross laughing all the way. Many will be the occasions when the response is made, 'As I was listening, I felt that the whole message was just for me.'

Where the Spirit is in operation, there will further be the sure evidence of *humility* and *mutual service*. Billy Graham has written:

> 'Renewal is brought by the Holy Spirit, and when He comes in all His power upon the Church, there will be clear evidences of the gifts and the fruit of the Spirit. Believers will learn what it means to minister to one another and build each other up through the gifts the Holy Spirit has given.'[2]

There is no mistaking whatever, when the Spirit of God is working in His reviving power. Then it is that the prayer warriors will murmur to each other, 'You know what? The tide is in.' Or as the Africans would put it, 'The rains are coming!'

> *'Fill me, Holy Spirit, fill me,*
> *More than fullness I would know:*
> *I am smallest of Thy vessels,*
> *Yet I much can overflow.'*

(A PRAYER FROM THE WELSH REVIVAL)

---

2 Billy Graham, *The Holy Spirit: Activating God's Power in your Life* (USA: Zondervan, 2002).

10

WHEN THE ENEMY
STRIKES BACK

'Nothing fails like success.'

(DEAN INGE OF ST PAUL'S CATHEDRAL,
LONDON: 1911–1934)

In 1994 the unthinkable happened in Rwanda, when genocide took over the country where the East African Revival had first begun. Here, it was the old curse of tribalism that proved to be the Enemy – with the mass killings of members of the Tutsi tribe by the more numerous Hutu. It is fair to say that the *balokele* ('the saved ones') of the revival were not involved in the killing spree. Sadly included among guilty partisans, however, had been members of the Roman Catholic priesthood, many of them having had a political stake in the then Tutsi-dominated government. For this, Pope Francis has since travelled to Rwanda, to make a full and formal apology on behalf of his Church.

In Rwanda's re-building, we must salute the ministry of many in the service of Christ who brought back the message of the Cross to bear once again upon millions of those with stricken consciences. Among such influential leaders have been African Enterprise's Antoine Rutayisire and John Kalenzi. Rwanda's steady recovery has been remarkable. But scars remain.

But – on another front – Festo again! In the great revival within the islands of Indonesia – the most populous Muslim nation in the world – it was Timor that was first embraced in the fervour of Christian expansion in 1965. But a scandal then broke out in the town of Soe, on the Eastern-most edge of Indonesia. There had been many manifestations of new life in the Spirit. In particular, it was reported that at a Holy Communion service, there was no wine, but that – in response to prayer – water had been turned into wine. The rejoicing was great. A problem arose when – in a vain attempt to repeat the miracle – the transformation had to be faked. A widespread scandal resulted, and it was decided to send for Festo Kivengere to fly in from East Africa, to give counsel.

He began by asking the chastened minister in charge: 'Brother, how many times in the New Testament did water turn into wine?'

'Oh – er – once.'

'Then why try and do it twice?'

Little by little, some of the hard lessons learnt earlier in East Africa were shared with these Christians of Indonesia.

In another country, a Christian leader came up to Festo and said, 'We *had* a revival.'

'*Had* one? What do you mean?'

The minister had had in mind certain unusual manifestations, but – now that they were over, the belief had taken hold that the revival was over too.

'But real revival is Jesus Christ Himself!' explained Festo. 'Don't think the manifestations were given to feed you! They shook you up so that you could go to the Bread of Life Himself!'

Then, in any awakening from God, every evangelist and every spiritual leader is exposed to the pressures of temptation – indeed to egotism, complacency and even financial cravings. Such can be the enticements that accompany power. Rarely has there been a more widespread and embracing revival than in the Korean Peninsula. Beginning first in 1907 in the North, it was hindered under Japanese domination, only then to be set back by Communist persecution. But it blossomed in the South – embracing millions – and today thousands of missionaries and evangelists from South Korea are preaching in many parts of the world.

It is hardly surprising that the powers of darkness are never inactive in the face of vast congregations and overflowing joy. Big 'Mega Churches' – led by a single dominant personality – are particularly fragile. In certain instances there emerged a Korean version of the 'prosperity gospel,' with the teaching – based on selective Bible texts – that a prayerful lifestyle will bring rewards both of health and wealth. A scandal of tax evasion on the part of one prominent leader emerged in February 2014, coupled with a conviction of embezzlement of many millions of dollars. Other leaders too, were caught up in similar scandals.

THE PROSPERITY GOSPEL

Indeed the outrageous 'prosperity gospel' – perpetrated largely from the West – has penetrated into some of the greatest areas of Christian growth in the developing world, not least in India, Africa and South America. Its proponents will quote Deuteronomy 28:11, 'And the Lord will make you abound in prosperity.' Then follows a reference to Hebrews 7:22. 'Jesus is the mediator of a better covenant.' The argument then runs, 'If it was the will of God for men and women to prosper *then,* how much more so, under the *New* Covenant!' Try preaching that in Bangladesh, in Haiti – or in Nairobi's shanty town of Kibera!

But are we surprised? We have only to read the Acts of the Apostles to learn of similar occurrences, as in the case of Ananias and his wife Sapphira, whose greed over a piece of property placed them under the condemnation that they had not lied to men, but to God. Such an act could not live in the white-hot purity of the new infant church following Pentecost, and the two offenders 'fell down and died' much to the distress and fear of the whole church (Acts 5:1-11).

A colleague who had accompanied the Apostle Paul and his trusted companion Luke on their perilous journeys had, at one stage, been Demas. But material allurement eventually took Demas out of the action, for – as Paul wrote to his protégé Timothy, 'Demas hath forsaken me, having loved this present world and is departed ...' (2 Tim. 4:10 KJV).

THE UNDERMINING OF THE TRUTH

There is also theological liberalism – with its tenuous views on Scripture – so offering a further weapon to the Enemy's armoury. Oradea – the second largest city in

Romania – became a scene of great revival during the Pastorship of Paul Negrut – leader of the Second Baptist Church, then the largest congregation in Europe. Tortured by the communists for his beliefs, during the hideous Ceaucescu regime, Paul was eventually to make a visit to the United Kingdom. In London he met with church leaders and theologians, some of whom were of a certain 'revisionist' outlook.

Having heard Pastor Paul speak and preach, they remonstrated with him for his strong belief in the inerrant truths of inspired Scripture. He met them by replying, 'Don't you realize? Many of us in Romania have been tortured for these beliefs. Numbers of us have died. And now you tell us that there was no need to have believed in all those teachings in any case!' He added, 'Would you think that *your* beliefs are such that you would die for them?'

To be true, the physical opposition and rioting faced by preachers across the ages will provide stiff challenges enough – but they are not entirely unexpected. The mobs that John and Charles Wesley faced at St. Ives and Falmouth during the eighteenth century were as rugged in spirit as the rocky coastline at Land's End, but the two brothers could take such batterings as they received in their stride.

More subtle, by far, is what the New Testament makes clear – that the greatest menace to the faith of Christ crucified and risen, arose not from the threats of imperial Rome nor indeed from militant Judaism. Rather they came – and always come – from false teachers within the church itself who *'having a form of godliness but denying its power ... are the kind who worm their way into homes and gain control ... always learning but never able to acknowledge the truth'* (2 Tim. 3:1-9).

This is where the danger has always existed from the
very beginning; from within the church itself. The English
Bible translator and scholar, J.B. Phillips, once declared:

> 'But I say quite bluntly that some of the intellec-
> tuals (by no means all, thank God!), who write
> so cleverly and devastatingly about the Christian
> faith, appear to have no knowledge of the living
> God. For they lack awe, they lack humility, and
> they lack the responsibility which every Christian
> owes to his weaker brother. They make sure they
> are never made "fools for Christ's sake", however
> many people's faith they may undermine.'[1]

THE EXAGGERATION OF THE TRUTH

By contrast with the undermining of the truth, every genuine spiritual awakening can be beset with the inclination
to over-emphasise a valued blessing of the Holy Spirit,
and go over the top with it, so causing confusion and even
something of a sectarian 'movement' that pulls God's
saints away from the main line of Christ's Church.

Let us take some instances from Heshbon Mwangi, a
major leader of the Revival in Kenya. We had come to know
this perceptive Kikuyu pastor when he became godfather to
my brother Peter. Heshbon – as he looked back over fourteen years of the revival – pointed out that not a year went
by without some 'satanic attack' being launched upon the
church, and each time by way of a different emphasis. Con-
cerning one year, he wrote, 'The Evil One came as an angel
of light, bringing visions of the Cross and of 'The Lord' to

---

1 J.B. Phillips, *Ring of Truth: A Translator's Testimony* (UK: Hodder and Stoughton, 1967), pp. 7-8.

one and another of the more earnest ones, making them pin their faith to these outward and visible physical manifestations, instead of trusting only in the precious Blood of the Lamb. Many of these were lost to Mau Mau terrorism.'

Of another year, Heshbon wrote, 'This year Satan worked in this way, that when some met for fellowship, they spoke much of dreams and visions, and had controversies about such things as the eating of pork, and of lying prophecies that the Europeans would be put out of their homesteads; that these would be given to the saved.'

Heshbon continued, 'This year Satan made war along these lines: he caused the preachers to weep, and so caused weeping in the gatherings. People thought that they had been saved by these signs of emotion but they were not delivered from sin. Emotion is not salvation.' Another year: 'Satan deceived people into listening and waiting in passivity for the filling and guiding of the Holy Spirit. By this means, people were deceived into listening to evil spirits. The evil spirits threw people on the ground, causing them to feel burning sensations, and making them thirsty; some destroyed their possessions. Brethren, if someone is saved, there is nothing greater than to have the Lord Jesus in us.'

Such accounts might have been written by John Wesley 200 years earlier in his journals, where he quotes from a colleague, Mr. Evans:

'It is common in the congregations for anyone that has a mind to give out a verse of an hymn. This they sing over and over with all their might, perhaps above thirty, yea, forty times. Meanwhile the bodies of two or three, sometimes ten or twelve, are violently agitated, and they leap up and down, in all manner of postures, frequently for hours together.'

Wesley concludes, 'These are honest, upright men who really feel the love of God in their hearts. But they have little experience, either of the ways of God or the devices of Satan. So he serves himself of their simplicity in *order to wear them out* and to bring a discredit on the Work of God'.[2]

On another level the Apostle Paul could discern when certain supernatural manifestations were not of the Holy Spirit, but rather from below. On his first visit to Europe he was to encounter a young prophetess who would follow the Apostles with her cry, 'These men are servants of the Most High God, who are telling you the way to be saved.' Yet Paul was eventually perceptive enough to recognise that behind such apparently supportive utterances lay an evil spirit that had to be commanded to depart (Acts 16:16-18).

Perhaps we can sum up the marks of false teaching that have hindered the reviving work of the Spirit right up to the present day. Again and again what has been promoted is what we may call:

THE JESUS-PLUS MESSAGE

In Paul's day it was so often 'faith in Jesus' *plus* the tagging on of Jewish procedures, including Jewish male circumcision. In recent times we have been presented with a *Political* Messiah, or – as in the days of the Crusades – with a *Military* Christ – or, through liberal teaching, with a *Social-programme* Christ. Show business offered us a *Superstar* Christ. Postmodernism gave us a *Designer* Christ, of your own devising! Indeed, as the Episcopal Bishop of

2 August 27, 1763, in *Wesley His Own Biographer* (London: C.H. Kelly, 1891),
   p. 324.

Pennsylvania, Charles Bennison, once asserted, 'We wrote the Bible; we can rewrite the Bible!'

But another line of departure we may entitle:

THE WE-THEM SYNDROME

The Christian church today can be warned by the bragging super-apostles of Paul's day who only saw precious souls as fodder for their own ego. The tendency is quite common today. It is the approach: 'If *we* put on *that* piece of music; if *we* set the worship-stance, language, and style in *this* way, it will make *them* – out there – respond in *that* desirable way.' This is where manipulation begins.

Such a stance is evidenced in such simple language as, 'Hey, we've got a great line-up for you tonight!' ... 'Now what we want you to do is turn to your neighbour and say "I love you!"' or – as I heard once, 'If you love Jesus, I want you now just to get out your keys and rattle them for him!'

On the altogether more serious level, what was it that Paul's 'super-apostles' were after? Why, it was to take, capture and hold those new believers in Asia Minor *tightly within their own outfit*. This was their aim, and this was their boast, every time they smelt success.

'Poor old Paul!' they would smile to each other. 'We're steadily taking over! Heard the latest? We've now got Corinth! And – there are other churches he's started that are now carrying our DNA!'

We have seen this in recent years, when 'heavy shepherding' has taken over a church – led by very authoritarian leadership. The whole ridiculous rigmarole begins to fall apart, once a discerning follower of Jesus recognises, 'No; I'm a disciple of ... One Man Only.' A third approach that can create division within a revival may be entitled:

THE POWER-MAD PROGRAMME

Power ... health ... money – that is enough to strip the real power out of revival. It was never the way Jesus lived; nor any of His apostles. We think of John, banished by the Romans to a cave; of Thomas, devoting himself to India; of James, killed by the sword; of Paul, basketed out of Damascus.

Astonishingly people were – and still are – taken in by some of those strange TV religious programmes, in which the whole 'show' – peppered with manipulative demands for money – has been carefully choreographed from beginning to end. When genuine revival blessing comes – and the enemy strikes back – we understand better Paul's thrice-used word, 'masquerading'... .

'For such men are false apostles, deceitful workmen, masquerading as apostles of Christ. And no wonder for Satan himself masquerades as an angel of light. It is not surprising, then, if his servants masquerade as servants of righteousness. Their end will be what their actions deserve' (2 Cor. 11:13-15).

'I hear those TV preachers;
Holy-get-you-rich-quick teachers,
Like pre-digested TV dinners,
Offer instant salvation packs for sinners;
'Put your hand on the TV screen'
Makes God look like a slot machine.
Is this really what You meant?
By your costly blood-bought Covenant?'

(FROM AN ALBUM BY GARTH HEWITT)

11

'TUKUTENDEREZA!'

'The people are the meeting, not the preacher.'[1]

Bible students have sometimes wondered why, in the New Testament, there were very few 'commands' given to the fledgling church to go out and *evangelise*. True, we have our Lord's parting commission to 'go and make disciples of all nations' but we comb almost in vain for similar directives elsewhere.

The reason comes in terms of what amounted to *the Announcement of an Event* – followed by *an Explosion of Joy*. There was no stopping the running feet on the day of Christ's resurrection from the dead. The good news simply had to be spread! Then, from Pentecost onwards, the dispersion of the 3,000 – and plenty more – amounted to an involuntary desire to tell the dying world of new life, available to all, in Christ. The new believers needed little command to go and tell! They were captivated by a confidence and exuberance that was infectious in its appeal.

---

1 William Stead et al., *The Welsh Revival* (Trumpet Press, 2015).

Rejoicing *and songs* accompanied their testimonies – from Jerusalem to Joppa!

> 'Speak to one another with psalms, hymns and spiritual songs. Sing and make music in your heart to the Lord, always giving thanks to God the Father for everything, in the name of our Lord Jesus Christ' (Eph. 5:19-20).

By contrast to the virtual absence of corporate singing in most of the mainline world religions, Christianity is a belief-system that, more than not, is identified by its songs!

MUSIC PROVIDES A KEY TO THE UNIVERSE

Again and again in Scripture, the glowing truth is underlined for us that, from the beginning of the universe, music was woven into the very fabric of Creation. When – in perhaps the oldest book of the Bible – the suffering Job sought an answer to his problems, he was met by the divine counter-question: 'Where were you when I laid the earth's foundation ... or who laid its cornerstone – *while the morning stars sang together and all the angels shouted for joy?'* (Job 38:4,6). Music is evidently integrated with the Creation itself.

It was the appearance and the singing praises of the angels of God that arrested the shepherds of Bethlehem, the night that Jesus was born. It was the Apostle John in his exile at Patmos who heard the praises of numerous angels as they sang: 'Worthy is the Lamb who was slain, to receive power and wealth, and wisdom and honour, and glory and praise!' The praises continued universally until the four living creatures said, 'Amen,' and the heavenly elders fell down and worshipped!

Michael Lawson – a Christian of Jewish background – was once a colleague of mine in central London. Immersed in music – and professionally trained as a performer – he confided to me that his departure from atheism was prompted by an inner query: *From where has this astonishing world of music originated?* This led to his subsequent discovery of life in Christ, while at Sussex University.

Music is a legacy bequeathed to us from the very beginning. On one level alone, it possesses power to attract and excite thousands of avid devotees, in festivals at Glastonbury, Montreux or Austin, Texas. It can – of course – be distorted, abused and even demonized. But in the hands of a George Frederick Handel, or a Beethoven, it rises to heights of majesty with symphonies and oratorios that fill the great auditoriums and concert halls of the world.

MUSIC PROVIDES WINGS TO THE TRUTH

When music is aligned decisively with the Christian gospel, the sky is the limit! To Noel Tredinnick – for many years director of music at London's All Souls Church – is owed the gratitude of churches worldwide that have benefited from his seminars on the enhancing of their music. 'The Word always comes first!' Noel would exclaim. 'But the music is there as its vital handmaid.' Thus, when the music and the proclaimed word are fused together – as in the celebrated All Souls 'Prom Praise' programmes in the Royal Albert Hall – the overall effect is massive. Particularly has this been so, with Noel deliberately featuring music that originates with the natural genius of the created order, yet running alongside specifically 'Christian' music. Aaron Copland's thumping celebration of the American West in '*Hoe Down*' may be followed by Nigel Swinford's

Christ-inspired *'Marriage at Sunrise'* – sung by a dedicated soloist. When a ninety-piece orchestra backs a large
gathered choir, under a conductor who 'preaches' his way
through the programme, there we have it – and it begins
to make me wonder wistfully, *With music like this, maybe the day will come when we can turn London into a
church!*

It is the very alliance of music with the gospel which –
on virtually every level – has set revivals alight; not least
in Africa and Korea ... and how the people love to sing!
Thus, while music gives wings to the Truth, it also provides something further:

MUSIC PROVIDES TRUTH WITH A HOME

Sweeping across all America at the height of his power,
D.L. Moody knew well that the messages he was thun-
dering out would find a permanent lodging-place in the
hearts of his listeners, once the teaching could be set to
memorable music that the crowds could hum as they set
off home. Moody once addressed delegates at a great conference with the words: 'I want to make as much of music
as possible here. Music and the Bible are the two important agencies with which to reach the world, and I've made
as much of singing as I have of preaching.'

Like the Wesleys before him, Moody was aware that
the best hymns tell of the great saving actions of God and
that the setting of Gospel truth to music was the surest
way of locking the Christian world-view into the corporate memory of a church and even an entire nation.

He also knew the power of a tune to stir emotions.
Indeed, when he once asked his daughter-in-law to play
'Rock of Ages' on the piano, she sat down and began – with

slow soulful chords – to play 'Yankee Doodle' – and then
watched fascinated as the tears rolled down Moody's
cheeks.

A CHURCH'S ACID TEST

True, there have been periods in Christian circles when
songs and hymns have descended to what the Danish phi-
losopher Søren Kierkegaard would have described as 'lu-
dicrous twaddle'. Indeed, the banal music and repetitive
words in certain fellowships at the present time – both
in Britain and America – stand a fair chance of destroy-
ing evangelical worship altogether. The acid test of any
church is whether its 'regulars' have the confidence to in-
vite their unbelieving neighbours along, and to know that
they will not be bemused or embarrassed by creepy inaudi-
ble prayers in language laced with clichés and meaningless
acronyms – let alone 'performance' songs with unknown
and unpredictable tunes that jump around and leave them
stranded. And then it was Voltaire who made the observation of the lyrics alone: '*If a thing is too silly to be said, it
can always be sung.*'

Singing – and even the chanting of slogans – can
become mindless when the corporate mentality of a
crowd has completely lost its way. It was a BBC producer, John Forest, who was attending a Christian rally
where slogans and 'Jesus shouts' were being repeated
endlessly. Finally John took the initiative in one shout
of his own:

'Give me an R!' he cried.

'R!' came the responsive chant from the crowd.

'Give me an H!' he yelled.

'H!' they all cheered with spiritual devotion.

Methodically the producer shouted his way through the word he had chosen … until suddenly the crowd realized what word they were mindlessly chanting. It was R H U B A R B.

The evangelist John Chapman of Sydney Australia once told me, 'No, I'm sorry to say I hate worshipping in that church.'

'Oh my,' I replied. 'What's the matter with it, Chappo?'

'Well,' came the reply; 'until the sermon itself, the whole event is an exercise in studied mediocrity.'

SONGS THAT TOUCH THE HEART

By contrast, we may bless Heaven for evangelists, pastors and song writers around the world who know their way around both music and the Bible. Theirs is the ability to come up with worship songs that can touch the heart – and raise the roof. Among them have been Graham Kendrick, Michael W. Smith, Keith and Kristyn Getty and Stuart Townend. And we are quick to add Tim Hughes, the Fellinghams, Chris Tomlin and Amy Grant … and these are but a handful. I have been honoured myself to work in fellowship with Timothy Dudley-Smith, Michael Baughen, Chris Idle, John Barnard, Ken Habershon and Joel Payne … and that is to leave out Noel Tredinnick!

The great hymns of earlier years by such as Isaac Watts, Fanny Crosby, John Newton and Richard Baxter would later prove to be a sure-fire weapon against error, when the critical modernist theology from Germany began to pour its way into the world towards the close of the nineteenth century. At that time evangelical theology had yet to find its feet, and would have been helpless against the tide of critical unbelief – but for the hymns! Even now, the singing saves the day in many western liberal churches, where the old traditional hymns effectively counter every limp dissertation from the pulpit – serving meanwhile to keep a glimmer of spiritual vitality alive.

PREACHING TO THE MINERS

As for the Wesleys – having been banished from the pulpits and buildings of the Established Church – John and Charles were timidly about to take to preaching in the fields – 'a mad notion' as John declared. Timorously, on Hannam Mount at Northfields, near Bristol, Charles sang and John preached; beginning with an audience solely composed of local miners … and then watched the 'white gutters made by their tears down their black cheeks'.

During the fifty-year revival that lay ahead, the Wesleys represented what Stanley Ayling describes as 'a religion not so much for the people as of the people.'[2] When that happens, we have a revival!

So, at times we can forget the preacher! The songs that accompany the message ensure that the truths proclaimed are then stamped upon the memory of countless thousands, often for life. Moody's accomplice and soloist for many years was Ira D. Sankey. Most of his songs and solos were so written and composed that they could easily and quickly be picked up by an entire congregation. The words conveyed luminous Bible truth, and the melodies were immediately accessible. Indeed, in the single year of 1875, more people heard the gospel songs of Sankey than listened to the music of Beethoven during the entire nineteenth century. Similarly, America's 'Beloved Gospel

---

2 Stanley Ayling, *John Wesley* (HarperCollins, 1979).

Singer' George Beverly Shea sang 'live' to more people in his lifetime than Frank Sinatra.

Nowhere has the power of Christian song been more effective than in Africa, where rhythm and beat are part of the indigenous psyche. When entire Masai villages were turning en masse to the Christian faith in the 1960s, the Bible teaching on Sunday would be converted into brand new songs ready for the following week – set to their own rhythmic jingles as they danced and stamped with joy.

The infectious power of attraction – emitted from the joyous singing fellowships united in the same love – was brought home to me by reports coming from South Sudan. Typically, a group of Sudanese believers would be sitting around a fire in the open air, after the sun had gone down. Testimonies of blessing would be shared, verses from Scripture would be exchanged, and exclamations of joy would intersperse the proceedings. Further away in the darkness, however, would be the unseen Watchers, of other beliefs, listening … and entranced. As the evening progressed, one or other would, yard by yard, noiselessly begin to approach the fire-lit scene. Slowly the distance would narrow, and before long, the visitor would be right by the fireside, incorporated into the beckoning circle of warmth, with still others following behind.

This is perhaps the most natural way in which a supernatural movement will grow – when those who see the Light from afar off become drawn in to the family of faith by a fellowship of men and women *'who shine like stars in the universe as they hold out the word of life'* (Phil. 2:14-15).

We have saved *the* song of the East African Revival – 'Tukutendereza' – for the end of this chapter. I have heard

it – and sung it myself – many hundreds of times, in
Rwanda, Uganda, Kenya, Tanzania and even Zimbabwe.
Simple in the extreme, it runs:

> *'Tukutendereza Yesu,*
> *[We praise you, Jesus,]*
> *Yesu Mwana, Gw'endiga;*
> *[Jesus the Lamb;]*
> *Omusayi gwo gunaziza,*
> *[Your Blood cleanses me,]*
> *Nkwebaza omulokozi!*
> *[I thank you, Saviour!]'*

12

REVIVAL'S HARVEST

*'I read in a Book that a man called Christ went
about doing good. It is very disconcerting that
I am so satisfied with just going about.'*

(TOYOHIKO KAGAWA –
JAPANESE EVANGELIST: 1888–1960)

There he was – in the semi-final of the 2015 Rugby World
Cup – Adam Ashley-Cooper of Australia, scoring the
second of his three brilliant tries against Argentina. Pam
had her camera at hand and managed to snap him as he
threw himself over the line with his index finger raised in
triumph.

Then, tracing his background, we discovered that Ashley-Cooper's name went back more than 150 years to *another* Ashley Cooper; a Londoner, from whom Adam is
directly descended. Of *this* Ashley Cooper it may be said
that he represented a direct follow-on from the Wesleyan
Revival, having been born just ten years after the death
of John Wesley. He became a British Parliamentarian in

1826 – known as the 7th Earl of Shaftesbury. But his fame was not due to his aristocracy. Nor was he rich, a celebrity, or a gigantic personality. He simply became loved and honoured because – as a Christian believer – he put all his energies into alleviating the lives of deprived people.

'THE POOR MAN'S EARL'

His was the era of *Oliver Twist* – with its orphans and widows, of the chimney boys who spent most of their day forced into darkness as they cleaned chimney after chimney; of the mentally ill – trapped in the degrading and disgusting conditions of the lunatic asylums. Ashley Cooper took the part of boys and girls of eight, nine and ten, obliged to work from dawn till night in the factories. He looked to the interests of the miners and those with no work and hopeless prospects. He pushed bill after bill through Parliament; *The Factory Act, Lunacy Acts, the Mines and Colliery Acts, the Chimney Sweepers Act* and plenty more. He would welcome the poor into his home. He would put on parties for East Enders, and indeed – every time he went visiting in the East End – the children would rush out, crowding around him as their friend.

Committed to world evangelisation, he involved himself with many missionary societies, and was President of the British and Foreign Bible Society. Eventually, Ashley Cooper died in 1885. As his coffin was being drawn along for the service in London's Westminster Abbey, the streets were lined with young people, factory workers, bootblacks, flower girls and sweepers – paying their respects to 'The Poor Man's Earl'.

Eventually, in the very centre of London, at Piccadilly Circus, a memorial, mounted above a fountain, was put up in Ashley Cooper's memory by a grateful nation. The renowned statue of Eros – featuring a boyish figure with a bow and arrow – was to become famous, not far from 'Shaftesbury Avenue', and the nearby 'Shaftesbury Theatre'. The next time you are in the area, buy yourself – at the very least – a tea towel, featuring a tribute to a man who had emerged from Revival time.

THE RETURN OF CHRIST

What motivated him supremely was the message of Christ's final Return. Towards the end of his life he said, 'I do not think that in the last forty years I have lived one conscious hour that was not influenced by the thought of our Lord's return.'

Can we expect anything different, when looking for evidence that a spiritual awakening has taken place? Writing about America's Second Great Awakening of 1800, Dr. Tom Phillips gives us the quoted remarks from George Baxter of Kentucky, in the aftermath of the revival:

> 'The most moral place I have ever seen … a religious Awe seemed to pervade the country … something extraordinary seemed necessary to arrest the attention of a giddy people who were ready to conclude that Christianity was a fable. This revival has done it!'[1]

Social reform – in a previously godless society – has always closely followed movements of revival. This is evident from Scripture. While 'Revival' may not be the most accurate word to describe certain Old Testament renewals

---

[1] Tom Phillips, *Jesus Now* (Broadstreet Publishing Group, LLC, 2016), p. 73.

of the covenant faith, *awakenings* there certainly were! We have already noted this with regard to Josiah's reforms (2 Chron. 34-35). To that we may add the comprehensive spiritual restoration immediately following the rise of King Hezekiah, son of the idolatrous Ahaz (2 Chron. 9-31). And there are plenty more.

SOCIAL REFORM

Characteristic of Judah's own renewal at the time of her restoration from exile was the aspect of social reconstruction – under Ezra and Nehemiah – relating to the restoration of Jerusalem's laws, temple and walls.

Forward the video a little! A true revival is characterized by its accompanying social and moral effect upon society. A supreme example of this is evidenced in the impact made through the work of such inheritors of Britain's evangelical revival as John Venn of the 'Clapham Sect' and William Wilberforce, champion abolitionist of the slave trade.

Of 1829, the English social reformer Francis Place wrote, 'I am certain I risk nothing when I assert that more good has been done to the people in the last thirty years than in the three preceding centuries; that during this period they have become wiser, better, more frugal, more honest, more respectable, more virtuous than they ever were before.'[2] For this transformation, the Wesleys – under God – were partly responsible. Further, however, the members of Venn's Clapham Sect built on Wesley's foundations, bringing their influence to bear in those circles which the Methodist revival could not easily hope to reach.

---

2 M.J. Quinlan, *Victorian Prelude: A History of English Manners 1700–1830* (Columbia University Press, 1941), p. 173.

As for Venn, to him is greatly credited the campaign for vaccination against smallpox, and in 1806 for the first time London recorded a whole week without a single death from the contagion. The Clapham group were also behind moves to give Roman Catholics the vote. Michael Hennell quotes Venn: 'Godliness is not a cold assent to the truths of religion: it is not a natural softness and benevolence of temper: it is not the abstaining from gross sins, or the giving to God a part of our hearts ... no, godliness is the entire subjection and devotedness of the soul to God himself.' [3]

HANNAH MORE'S TRACTS

A noted ally of the Clapham sect was educational pioneer, playwright, social reformer and dedicated evangelical, Hannah More – a member of London's fashionable 'Blue Stocking Club' – and adored by scores of aristocratic men. She was among the leaders in recognizing the need for schools to reach every level of society, and indeed founded the *More Schools* in the mining villages of England's West country. A staunch anti-Jacobite – and horrified by the violence following the French Revolution across the English Channel – she wrote scores of moral, religious and occasionally political tracts, simple pamphlets aimed at the everyday English reader. They became known as Hannah More's *Cheap Repository Tracts*. They were written, partly, to counter Tom Paine's *The Rights of Man* (1791) with its call for revolution and the end of monarchy. One of the Clapham Sect – a prominent banker, Henry Thornton – acted as Hannah's treasurer. As Jeremy and Margaret Collingwood of Bristol were to write, 'The tracts

---

3 Hennell, p. 205.

consisted of ballads, Sunday readings and stories, some of which were serialized; and they were generally illustrated by lively wood-cuts ... By March 1796, only one year after the commencement of the scheme, over two million copies of the tracts had been distributed, and it is safe to assume that the final sales of the tracts were at least two or three times that number.[4] Such titles as *The Story of Sinful Sally* and *Black Giles the Poacher* became known across England at a time when the population numbered only nine million.

Turn the Carpet was a tract featuring a philosophical conversation between two carpet weavers. It began:

'This world which clouds thy soul with doubt
Is but a carpet inside out.'

The poem ends:

'Then shall we praise what here we spurn'd,
For then the carpet shall be turn'd.'

So great was the impact of Hannah More's tracts that it was even suggested she had written them at the request of the Prime Minister, William Pitt. It was also reckoned that some of her output had helped to check 'a very formidable riot' in Bath.

THE WORLD'S MOST INFLUENTIAL CHURCH

Hannah More was but one of many who responded to the remarkable leadership exercised worldwide by the Clapham group. It could be argued that by the beginning of the nineteenth century, Holy Trinity Clapham had become the most

---

4 Jeremy and Margaret Collingwood, *Hannah More* (Lion Books, 1990).

influential church in the world. In the words of Professor Harold Perkin: '*Between 1780 and 1850 the English ceased to be one of the most aggressive, brutal, rowdy, outspoken, riotous, cruel and bloodthirsty nations in the world ...*'[5]

In the wake of every revival we can discern a variety of positive effects. And we can trace this pattern in any country of the world wherever the Christian gospel has taken a leap forward. When visiting the Hombolo Leprosy Centre in Tanzania, I encountered the redoubtable Irish medical researcher and cancer specialist, Dennis Birkett, discoverer of the *Birkett's Lymphoma*. For me it was the beginning of a long friendship. On leprosy, he commented, 'I've travelled all over the tropics, and inevitably, on reaching any leprosy settlement, I know full well that those running it will invariably be Christians.'

Thankfully leprosy is now diminishing worldwide, but it has been a longtime curse of civilizations. It is supremely to the actions and example of Christ that we owe the self-giving of missionary doctors and their companions, in the centuries-long effort to alleviate this dreaded disease. Dr. June Morgan, of the Overseas Missionary Fellowship, has testified that the church of the Far East region where she worked owed its early origin entirely to leprosy patients who had come to faith. 'No one else would touch them,' she affirmed.

MINISTRY AND HEALING

I saw it for myself, when taken by Dr. Leonard Sharp to Bwama Island, on beautiful Lake Bunyonyi in South West Uganda. There he had founded a leprosy settlement – with

---

5 As quoted in John M. MacKenzie in Tom Griffiths (ed.), *Ecology and Empire: Environmental History of Settler Societies* (Keele University Press, 1997).

its hospital, school and church. The Ugandan Revival was then at its height. Christian ministry and healing went hand in hand within this community which was to rise to over 1,000 in number. Many were the shining testimonies of salvation received, as patients affirmed their gratitude at having been brought to Bwama, where the love of Jesus was so strongly in evidence. And when Sunday arrived, the thump of the drums could be heard across the lake – accompanied by the joyful singing of gospel hymns and *'Tukutendereza'*. Later years have seen the grateful closure of the settlement, as it is no longer needed.

In the mention of 'healing', this too is a blessing that can come out of the direct proclamation of the gospel. One of my earlier friends in Africa has been one-eyed Orpheus Hove of Zimbabwe. He was a prominent leader within African Enterprise – combining evangelism with humanitarian aid in the cities of Africa. I asked him one day, 'How do you see healing fitting into all this, Orpheus?'

'Oh, very simply!' he smiled. 'Not that we are anything other than a *Gospel* mission. So, when I have been leading one of my own campaigns, we have never advertised it as a 'Come-and-get-healed' mission. We are simply preaching Jesus.

'But,' he went on, 'sometimes while I am preaching, somebody may suddenly get healed! These things can happen here in revival times, especially when – as is often the case – there's no medical support around.'

LILIAN CLARKE

Another long-term AE colleague was Lilian Clarke, a British missionary who seemed to know every blade of grass on the rolling hills of Uganda. She had worked in evangelism with Festo Kivengere, supporting mission after mission. She described a miraculous healing she had witnessed one Sunday.

'It was simply a little Gospel meeting,' she remembered. 'There we were – Festo and I – in what can only be described as a very basic Ugandan mud-bricked building, where *church* was going on.'

Festo filled in the details. 'It was not a healing meeting. It was a little Gospel service, with some twenty-five people meeting for worship, singing and sharing God's Word. A man, crippled from birth, was sitting by the door. He had never walked. He crawled in for the service as usual. As the meeting went on, he was overcome by the message. With tears streaming down his cheeks he said, 'I want to accept the Lord Jesus.'

'One of the leaders said, 'Get up and accept him!'

'The cripple got up – legs and all – to the amazement of the Christian who had told him to! He told us all how God had liberated him, and forgiven him his sins. Then, towards the end, he looked down at his legs and said, 'And, as if that were not enough, he has made my legs well!' Later we gave this man a lift in our car, and saw him walking home. He is still known today. It was a real New Testament miracle, but our joy was not for his straightened legs; he was bound to die later on. We were rejoicing over the miracle of the New Life – never to die again! That is the greatest miracle ...'

When God is marching on, it seems that he will scoop up anybody who is open to the Call – from a Wesley or an Ashley Cooper, to a John Venn, a Dennis Birkett, a Hannah More, an Orpheus Hove or a Lilian Clarke. And what shall I more say? I do not have time to tell about

George Muller who gave his life for the orphans; Selena, the generous Countess of Huntingdon, John Nicholson and Will Knights with The Gideons, the New York merchant and philanthropist William E. Dodge, or Robert Raikes who founded the Sunday School movement ... *the world was not worthy of them!*

> 'One drop of water helps to swell the ocean;
> a spark of fire helps to light the world.
> None are too small, too feeble, too poor to be of service.
> Think on this and act.'

(HANNAH MORE: 1745–1833)

13

CAN YOU SPOT A
REVIVED CHURCH?

*'When the church of God uses the Apostolic
standard, it will be a praying church. That will be
its chief characteristic. These people prayed.'*

(FROM A SERMON BY GYPSY SMITH: 1860–1947)

'Tell me about your church!' I had just arrived for a conference on Christian evangelism, and he was the first delegate
I met as we queued up to register. 'Well,' came the smiling
reply, 'I'm from Cameroon, and I have my own church to
pastor. All that happened was that, one night in my area,
we put on an open-air showing of *The Jesus Film*. By next
morning we had a church! I've been its pastor ever since.'

It was a good start – and it helped to set the scene for
what followed over the next few days. *The Jesus Film* –
produced by Campus Crusade – is nominated in *The
Guinness Book of Records* as having been seen by more
viewers than any film in history. Professionally filmed, its

portrayal of the life of Jesus Christ has led to no less than 200 million professions of faith – and could be said to represent the single most powerful tool of evangelism in the twentieth century.

One film – and there we had it – a new church. Unimposing, perhaps, in its structure, but nevertheless bringing forty or fifty people under the shadow of the Cross, there to support, pray and sing with each other in a joyous attempt to witness to their surrounding region. This phenomenon is being multiplied worldwide at the present time.

AN UNCONTAINABLE CHURCH

In February 2017, Pam and I were visited by former Bible Society director James Catford and his wife Sue. After their recent visit to the Far East, we learnt that in China alone the Christian revival has escalated beyond all estimation. And none of it is 'big'. It is frequently through small gatherings, meeting in people's homes, that the wildfire-blaze of the Spirit has spread. There appears to have been very limited organization and little in the way of frontline leadership. Given the current ease of international travel, it is not surprising that many in the West are now encountering these new believers. It appears that the church in China is now uncontainable.

This is the wonder of how Europe itself was initially touched – first with a few women by the riverside in Philippi, next at the home of Lydia – a businesswoman; later with the house church meeting in the home of Jason in Thessalonica; later still at the home of Aquila and Priscilla in Corinth.

WHERE THE FRONT-LINE ACTION IS

It is not that we discount the great cathedrals or indeed the so-called mega-churches that can accommodate many thousands. They indeed serve us all, as effective and encouraging lighthouses of the faith. But in area after area, it is the smaller local church that represents the true front-line action.

Let us visit such a house-church meeting in the home of Mary, the mother of John Mark – evidently a close associate of the Apostle Peter. Many would gather there in the early stages of the New Testament church. Nevertheless, following the martyrdom of Stephen, the heat was on; it now being the turn of Herod Agrippa to attempt the crushing of the new movement. Heads were getting cracked, right and left.

Dispatching one of the precious and irreplaceable twelve Apostles with the sword – James, the brother of John – he next turned his attention to the Rock-man, Peter – clapping him into a top security jail, under heavy guard.

All the Herods of the Bible turned out to be bad. This one was Herod Agrippa the First. He was nephew to Herod Antipas, the murderer of John the Baptist. He was also a grandson of Herod the Great, who – in his massacring of the little children in Bethlehem – had hoped to destroy the infant Jesus.

This one – Agrippa – was a political man. And, as so often happens in history, the church was caught up in the tide of political events, and attacked by the actions of a political figure.

PRAYER CHANGES EVERYTHING

The political decision was a sound one. Execute one of the top three Apostles – James – and incarcerate the Number One man, with a view to having a 'show-piece' trial for the people in a few days' time; that was the ploy. But prayer changed all this.

> 'So Peter was kept in prison, but the church was earnestly praying to God for him' (Acts 12:5).

How little was that prayer gathering kept in the know! Since being arrested, was Peter perhaps already dead, like James? We are indebted to Luke, our meticulous historian, for giving us the full details of this entrancing episode.

Mary's house prayer-fellowship could have been a revival gathering in Uganda – at the height of the hideous regime headed by General Idi Amin. It could have been the home in Rwanda of a revival brother – one of my best friends in African Enterprise – Israel Havugamana. Israel was to be shot on the front path of his home by opponents, enraged by this champion of reconciliation.

Here, in Acts chapter 12, the people in Mary's house were praying, and Luke fills in the story for us. Over in the jail was Peter, sleeping between two soldiers, chained and inert, guarded by sentries. Then – with the shining of a bright light in the cell – comes the angelic visitation, the snapping of Peter's shackles, the silent opening of the gates as the angel escorts Peter past both oblivious guards, reaching the iron gate that, in turn, opens before them. Suddenly, at the end of the street, Peter is left alone.

At that point he makes straight for the church prayer meeting! It was the continuing, prevailing prayer that was the factor the authorities had never counted upon.

Consequently, Luke writes about the following morning with the masterly understatement that typified him: 'There was no small commotion among the soldiers over what had become of Peter.'

No small commotion! It was bedlam. The detainee had done a Houdini on the lot of them. And no one would ever know how it had been done. *But we know* – thanks to Luke's careful chronicling of the whole affair – and it seemed to have everything to do with prayer. It is not that prayer is in any way an insurance policy for a church facing adversity. Indeed, we do not turn to God primarily because we need Him, but because we love Him. The first sign of a new believer is that he or she begins to learn about prayer as a way of life; the events, big and little, the happinesses, the disasters and the boring 'in-between' periods as well.

The test of a true church can be made – as much as anything else – on the value it sets on its prayer life. 'Prayer is either a force, or a farce,' declared Joe Church. In this New Testament church of Acts, prayer seems to have been the touchstone; it is the test for so much.

PRAYER IS THE TEST OF OUR UNITY

'So Peter was kept in prison … *but* the church was earnestly praying to God for him.'

We do not read here that 'his friends were praying'. The statement is that *the church was at prayer*. Dedicated, prayerful agreement brought 'the Christians' together.

Here in this account, Herod believed that he had disposed of the church by shutting up its leader. But the church in Mary's house – by reason of its regular meetings for prayer – evidently was possessed of a background, a *reservoir* of prayer; they would pray whether there was a crisis or not, out of the love they had for their Lord. Thus, when the crisis burst upon them, there would have been that underlying confidence that God always hears, and always acts! Here was the test of their unity. We learn more, however.

PRAYER IS THE TEST OF OUR VITALITY

Every local church must face this. Imagine that your own church is in the Consultant's waiting room, when the buzzer goes, and, falteringly, we make our way through. Then comes the obvious first question as to our health: *'How are you?'* If we were living in the city of Smyrna – in Asia Minor – we would quickly be diagnosed as 'The Suffering Church'. Polycarp, one of our leaders, would indeed one day be scheduled for certain death. But we would also learn that, if we can endure, the winners' 'crown of life' will be ours – and that, despite the suffering, no evident defect is going to be registered on our record.

Alternatively, we might be the church from Pergamum, possibly facing surgery from 'the sharp double-edged sword' – but the reward for bravery will be a welcome diet of *covenant bread*.

If Thyatira was your church, the problem would be one of pollution – resulting from false teaching and immorality – but for which there could be available a unique 'morning star' return to recovery. If it had been Sardis, however, then – despite the outward healthy façade – the diagnosis would be, 'You are already virtually *dead*, suffering from the ailment we call "formalism".' But could we, perhaps, be jacked up again by a reviving U-turn, away from such approaching death?

If we were the Philadelphian church, we would seem to be on the way out altogether, but for three factors standing in our favour; a vital key, an open door and a stalwart pillar. Alternatively, if we were Laodicea, we are almost too proud to enter the waiting room at all, even though our actual state is one of pitiful poverty. The only way back is by welcoming the top Physician of souls through the church's door.

'So ... *how's the appetite – are you spiritually hungry? How's the pulse rate – does the heart of your church beat strongly to the message of the Cross? And now – let me test your breathing – how's the prayer life?*'

The Consultant's questions are all testing the health and vitality of the fellowship. His more detailed analysis of the situation can be checked in chapters 2 and 3 of the book of Revelation.

PRAYER IS THE TEST OF OUR RESOLVE

It would seem that – wherever the energizing power of the Spirit is at work, prayer will surge to the front – and stay there. Pete Greig is the instigator of the 24–7 Prayer movement which has reached more than half the nations on earth. He once told an enquirer: 'The vision is *Jesus*. You see bones ... but I see an *army!* It's part of the longing of creation itself, the groaning of the Spirit, the very dream of God' (Rom. 8:19-22).

Translate this into the local church! At the very least it surely means that the regular gathering for prayer will be, besides Sunday church, *the* central meeting of the entire week – on which day no other organization will be in action. All the church staff – together with council members and volunteer leaders – will be expected to gather, along with the entire fellowship. No 'rule' need be exerted about this! For, in this church of the Spirit, it will be the joy of God's people to come together for prayer. Here we must acknowledge that in many churches of the world, prayer of this kind is held *daily*.

There need be no artificial 'hype' when the church meets in this way. A true Spirit-filled church will come across as

Supernatural without being unnatural
Childlike without being childish
Authoritative without being manipulative
Prophetic without being chaotic

The reaction of the prayer gathering in Acts 12 is utterly typical. Peter is knocking at the door ... could this be an intruder? The soldiers? *Shall we send Rhoda along to investigate?* ...

'It's Peter! He's at the door!'

They couldn't believe it. Has the poor girl taken a turn? Can we get her a glass of water? 'And now – to the next topic! Let's just have some prayer for Herod ...'

Well, Rhoda persisted, and – finally, there was Peter.

Luke, again the master of understatement, simply reports, 'They were astonished.' Throughout Christian history this has been the delightful reaction of praying people. 'So, the Lord above was listening? Our prayer was *heard* – actually *heard!*' We find ourselves echoing Tennyson's words: 'More things are wrought by prayer than this world dreams of.'

When prayer is co-operating with the reviving Spirit of the Lord in any local church, the visitor from outside will be immediately aware of a different atmosphere,

a different expectation. A former member of another religion told me how it had affected her, when visiting the
church of St Peter's, Harold Wood, in England's county of
Essex. 'First,' she said, 'I had been attracted by the lifestyle
of a near neighbour of mine. Finally, I thought, I will go
to their place of worship on Sunday and see what it's all
about.'

'But,' she told me, 'I was scared to enter! As I came in
and sat down, I was terrified that holy people would come
up to me, smilingly eager, with shining eyes, to pull me in
to their religion. But it was all so ... *normal* ... even con-
versational. As I plucked up courage and looked around,
I could then recognise people I had seen in the supermar-
ket; down the road at the school gates. These were ordinary people – and yet, about the whole atmosphere in that
church, there was a magnetism I couldn't resist. I am so
happy to be one of them today.'

That is it: we can never *manufacture* such an 'atmosphere'. It is either there or not there! But when the love
of Jesus pulls men and women together as happened at
Mary's house , things will and do happen. And to God be
the glory!

*'Set yourself a target. Don't be content. Don't say 'Our
church is dull, the people have no vision.' It is your business to create the vision. This is part of your prayer life.
Go back and see if you can bring this to pass.'*

(ALF STANWAY OF MELBOURNE,
FORMER BISHOP IN TANZANIA)

14

CAN IT COME HERE?

'There seems to be a notion abroad that if
we talk enough and pray enough, revival will
set in like a stock market boom ...'

(A.W. TOZER)

It is utterly tantalizing. I have been to Cornwall, and gazed at the collapsed tin mine of Gwannap Pit where – as the fires of revival swept through Cornwall in the eighteenth century, John Wesley would stand before thousands of people assembled below him. I have stood by 'Whitefield's Mount' in London's south-east area of Blackheath, where George Whitefield would – with his cavernous voice – preach to 30,000 at a time. You can still visit Epworth Parish Church in Lincolnshire, where on 6th June 1742 John Wesley preached at his father's grave on the text: 'The kingdom of heaven is not meat and drink, but righteousness and peace, and joy in the Holy Ghost.'

I have visited Haworth in Yorkshire's West Riding, which itself became the centre of a great outpouring of

God's Spirit. The Reverend William Grimshaw began his ministry there in 1742. As an unconverted clergyman, he had first been arrested by *The Doctrine of Justification by Faith* – written by the Puritan, John Owen. From that time on, the fire began to fall. The difference to the preaching was such that a local clothier, Joseph Williams said, 'It was as though God had drawn up Grimshaw's Bible to heaven, and sent him down another!' An entry in the diary of a Yorkshireman named Burdsall read as follows after his first attendance at Haworth Church on New Year's Day in 1753:

> 'After waiting for a short time, a broad-set sharp-looking little man appeared, habited as a layman and buttoned up from the storm. He quickly loosed his garments. In a moment, he was in the pulpit and giving out a hymn; the people sang like thunder. His voice in prayer seemed to me as it had been the voice of an angel.'

'HE CARRIES FIRE'

John Wesley, who regularly preached for Grimshaw, once commented: 'A few such as him would make a nation tremble. He carries fire wherever he goes.'[1] Such fire inevitably brought the rage of drunken mobs upon the sturdy preacher. Often clubbed, bruised, and pelted with mud, he would continue to ride gamely on to his next preaching assignment. In his 'lazy week' he would preach some twenty times; in his 'busy week' he would preach from thirty to forty times. But of course, we must remember that he had no telephone and no emails to attend to!

---

1 Faith Cook, *William Grimshaw of Haworth* (Banner of Truth Trust, 1997).

When we read of mighty awakenings of God that have happened in the past, we might think it justifiable to question why such blessing may not occur again in our present time. Is the Christian landscape today to be coloured by an unsettling grey instead of blue skies and sunshine?

I remember once announcing to a group of lively children that I was going to show them a Tom and Jerry colour cartoon. Unfortunately the film distributors had posted to us the wrong film; it proved to be a black and white documentary of the British seaweed industry. The disappointment was, well, *palpable.*

RESURRECTION SUNRISE

Our calling today is to demonstrate to the apathetic and the cynical that life – far from being a never-ending grey documentary – is a lifetime adventure, lit up by the technicolor hues of Resurrection sunrise and confidence in the ascended rule of Christ.

And Revival in our time? If we tend to ask, 'How?' and 'Why?' we have only to turn to the Old Testament's last book – that of Malachi – for these words to have been echoed among the prophet's listeners. They express a series of charges put to the Lord God at a time of spiritual decline. They amount almost to accusations – but it is the Lord Himself who challenges these very questions.

If we follow the book's 'dialogue with God' through its four brief chapters, we can detect that – seven times in all – God's spelling-out of the spiritual state of His people is met by a counter-charge; by the question 'How?' – or 'Why?' ... *questions that effectively put God Himself into the witness box.* The distress of Malachi concerned the state of his fellow-patriots, for he recognised that – whatever message of the Lord was given them, they would continue to question and challenge it.

Yet at the start of the prophecy, the Lord's opening sentence to His people is, 'I have loved you' (Mal. 1:2). But the reluctance of Malachi's people to accept that statement is expressed in their immediate counter-question: 'How have you loved us?'

THE BREADTH OF 'ISRAEL'

If they had thought a little, they would have remembered the covenant with Abraham, the coming of the patriarchs, the deliverance from Egypt, the leadership of Moses and Joshua, of David, Solomon and the prophets; the Lord's presence with them in the mud flats of the exile; His destruction of Belshazzar's kingdom with the writing on the wall, the sending of Ezra and Nehemiah …

In the event, the prophetic answer focused simply on the choosing of Jacob as father of the nation, in preference to Esau (whose descendants were to become the Edomites – the hated enemies of Israel). God's choice of the people of Israel – beginning with Jacob – was that 'Israel' was ultimately broader than any ethnic or tribal group. As the Apostle Paul puts it perfectly, 'It is not the national children who are God's children, *but it is the children of the promise*' (Romans 9:8). Paul adds, 'It does not therefore depend on man's desire or effort, but on God's mercy' (v. 16).

We are reminded then that the very church of God – God's people – had begun – as Abraham was to realise – before 'Israel' had even existed! Seen in this bigger way, if a hated Edomite turned to the God of grace, then even an Edomite could become an 'Israelite'!

And that speaks to all humanity. The fact that I, as a Gentile, could enter Israel's sacred covenant of God through a side gate – where the Cross of Christ stood – is surely the great miracle of the gospel. Why, a Korean can enter the covenant, and so can a Pakistani, a New Yorker, or an Inuit!

CALLED, CHOSEN AND FAITHFUL

How do such know if they are chosen? Let them first learn that *Christ is THE supremely chosen One in whom God delights* (Isa. 42:1; 1 Pet. 2:4). So it only needs to be asked, 'Have *you* come to Christ – and are therefore identified as one of His own?' If the answer is *Yes,* then, because you are included as being 'in Him', you too are chosen! 'With Him will be His called, chosen and faithful followers' (Rev. 17:14).

Come back to Malachi. True, following the exile, the Jewish people had got their land back. They had even got their worship system back. 'But,' says the prophet, 'you're treating it like a *system*, a tired, mechanical performing of your service to God!' He continues, 'Another thing you do: you flood the Lord's altar with tears. You weep and wail because He no longer pays attention to your offerings or accepts them with pleasure from your hands. You ask, Why?'

Earlier, the priests – the ministers – are confronted by the words, 'And you say, "What a burden!"' The truth, however, is that it is the Lord who can become burdened by our threadbare service. The prophet puts it strongly with his words: 'You have wearied the Lord with your words.' And this – regarding the Lord who 'will neither slumber nor sleep' (Ps. 121:4).

A CAUSE OF WEARINESS

So, to the question, 'Can revival come here?' – we must be ready for what may be the Lord's tired response. It is indeed we servants and ministers in today's church who may ourselves be a cause of weariness – and even boredom – to the Lord, with the insulated 'empire-building' that can too easily describe our leadership and service. We can be those who would fail to hear Christ's response to our pleas, in the same way that we cannot accept advice or criticism from our own congregation or our colleagues. Like Malachi's priests, it is possible that we cannot absorb correction or any new thought, owing to our contentment simply to plough endlessly on with what we hug ourselves into believing is the 'ministry of the Word'. And ministry that has run out of Love – is a threadbare travesty. We will set out our glib 'visions for the future' before our weary members, urging an immediate and avid acceptance of them.

> 'Our mistake,' writes A.W. Tozer, 'is that we want God to send revival on our terms ... we want still to be in charge, guiding the chariot through the religious sky in the direction we want it to go, shouting 'Glory to God,' it is true, but modestly accepting a share of the glory for ourselves in a nice inoffensive sort of way. We are calling on God to send fire on our altars, completely ignoring the fact that they are our altars, and not God's... . Coldness, worldliness, pride, boasting, lying, misrepresenting, love of money, exhibitionism – all these things are practiced by professedly orthodox Christians, not in secret, but in plain sight, and often a necessary part of the whole religious show.'[2]

---

2 A.W. Tozer, *When Will Revival Come?*

We hear it everywhere: 'When is Revival coming? ... Oh if we could only have a national Revival!' Yet, I am sobered by the words of Joe Church when he wrote, 'To us European missionaries, this revival has been a searching experience, and most humbling. Time and again we have found that it is we who have hindered God's blessing. We had to be humbled to the dust.'[3]

The Pennsylvanian author and mission founder, James McConkey, has commented, 'It must be simple. God would not have made it difficult ... We take refuge in prayer, pleading, social service and giving our wealth. Thus we dodge the real issue.'[4]

This was precisely the problem confronting the prophet Malachi, then facing a spiritual temperature of zero, among the ministers of his time, the Levites. Told that they were 'robbing God' it is evident that their level of giving was the barometer of their spirituality at that time. It was shoddy and mean (Mal. 1:12-14). It often is!

At the height of the East African Revival a farmer brought to the wealthy Chief of his area ten cows.

'I have come for a purpose, sir,' said the man.

'What are those cows for?' asked the Chief.

'Sir, they are yours.'

'What do you mean – they are mine?'

'They are yours. When I was looking after your cattle, I stole two, and now they are eight, and I am bringing them.'

'Who arrested you?'

'Jesus arrested me, sir, and here are your cows.'

There was silence and no laughter.

---

3 J.E. Church, *Quest for the Highest* (Paternoster Press, 1981), p. 132.
4 James McConkey, *Court of Memory* (Dutton Books, 1983), p. 221.

A few days later an acquaintance of the Chief said to him, 'I hear you got eight free cows! You must be very happy!'

'Forget it! Since that man came, I can't sleep. If I want the peace he has, I'd have to return a hundred cows!'

The Chief resisted for fifteen years, and – indeed, when he finally surrendered to Christ – he had quite a lot to return!

Forget the tithes ... forget the cows ... The questions that we Christians in the West need to ask ourselves are, perhaps, three-fold:

ARE WE REALLY WANTING A REVIVAL?

The barometer of our spirituality may be different from that of Malachi's time. True, the prophet speaks of 'the Lord you are *seeking*' – a coming that would one day be announced by the Lord's 'messenger' – John the Baptist. But the question would be: 'Who can endure the day of his coming? Who can stand when he appears? For he will be like a refiner's fire or a launderer's soap. He will sit as a refiner and purifier of silver, he will purify the Levites ...' (Mal. 3:2-3). Question: Would such purification have been a welcome prospect for *the Levites* – the 'inside minis-ters' – who had so signally failed in their calling?

The year 2017 witnessed in Britain a number of ter-rible catastrophes in the first six months alone: terrorist attacks and killings on Westminster Bridge, in the Man-chester Arena, on London Bridge and in Borough Market, followed so soon after by an horrific fire which entirely destroyed a massive London tower block, killing scores of residents, many of them asleep in their beds. Utterly moving was the level of spontaneous loving support that flowed immediately from the surrounding communities, of all faiths and none. This, said Pam, as we watched the news, is *real* love in action. 'When the TV cameras have gone, these people will still be there, hard at it.'

Such love, at its best, is but a part of 'the river of the water of life, as clear as crystal, flowing from the throne of God and of the Lamb down the middle of the great street of the city' (Rev. 22:1, 2). Ultimately it is the love of Jesus. In the fourth century it was the Roman Emperor Julian who made the comment that the kindness of Christians shown to strangers was the principal cause of Christianity's great expansion. 'And this,' we often say, 'has to be practised.' No, it can't really be 'practised'. The greatest need of the church worldwide is to catch a fresh vision of Jesus Christ. Until that happens, churches can be cold and indifferent to one another, competitive, edgy and judgmental. How greatly would we desire the discerning power of the Spirit to come upon us? We could ponder a second question:

IF REVIVAL CAME, HOW WOULD THE CHURCHES COPE?

Could we manage with the welcoming, the understanding and harmonious integration required, with the flooding in of numerous outsiders into our churches – such as we are at present? What would such newcomers make of life in our fellowships? Here perhaps lies before us an exercise in *preparing the soil* for a visitation of the Holy Spirit.

IF REVIVAL CAME, ARE WE PREPARED TO FACE THE FIRE OF PERSECUTION?

For persecution there almost certainly would be. It has been so at other times. If a revival was to sweep across

the great conurbations of our era we would in all likeli-
hood run into a shoal of aggravation and opposition to
our teaching, our ethics, and our evangelism. Very possibly there would be imprisonments. Violent riots broke
out under the Wesleys in such places as Wednesbury and
St. Ives in Cornwall.

But those who have come through great awakenings
do not seem to have been too set back by the adversities,
religious or political. I quote – yet again! – Festo Kivengere.
Years ago, when being interviewed during a meeting at
the Keswick Convention, he told us all: 'Please don't be
shocked when you hear there's been a revolution in Uganda,
a revolution in The Congo, a revolution in Rwanda. These
are young countries, and this is Africa! It's exciting – as
exciting as Europe was three hundred years ago! Christianity
has never been afraid of revolutions – we are going to get
some more! But this does not mean that Christ has vacated
the Throne.'

'... *Satan can roar like a lion, but he has no authority to*
shake the Throne on which Jesus is sitting.'

(BISHOP FESTO KIVENGERE)

15

'BEGIN IT IN ME'

*'So many children of God are seeking an it as the
answer to their own need and that of the church;
an it which they have not as yet found.'[1]*

The evangelist Roy Hession, author of the best seller *Calvary
Road* was once accompanying Dr. Joe Church and William
Nagenda at a conference in Guebwiller, France. After the
meetings were over, William Nagenda took Roy quietly
aside and asked him a simple question: 'What is your vision?'
He waited patiently for an answer. Eventually Roy replied,
'I suppose I have got three visions. For years I have been an
evangelist, and I have this vision for evangelism still. And
now I am working in a society that is occupied with the
distribution of the Scriptures, and I have a vision for that
line of things too. Also – in view of this new experience
that has become mine – I have a vision for revival.'

As Roy Hession wrote later, 'William was deeply troubled over my answer, almost in despair over me. 'Brother,'

---

1 Roy Hession, *When I Saw Him* (Christian Literature Crusade, 1975)

he said, 'you have not really seen the way yet. A vision for evangelism, a vision for Scripture, and a vision for revival ... how terrible! There is only one vision, *and that is Jesus,* the Jesus you have been experiencing in revival. He includes everything.'[2]

Roy later described the prayer of Joe Church, on the occasion of their ministry together in the United States. Repeatedly, Joe Church's prayer was this: 'O God, give us just one man. If You give us just one man in America who has seen Jesus and known deeper brokenness at His Cross, then we can go home and say "Revival has come to America."'

LOVE THAT WINS THE WORLD

Ultimately true Christians are detected by the light and love of Jesus shining out of their eyes; by the humility of an attitude that focuses upon others, not upon themselves; by their gentleness of spirit, by the putting of themselves out for others – and their refusal ever to take revenge. It is love of this kind that wins the world. Frankly, someone filled with the love of Jesus will have little idea of the effect they have on others, simply because at heart they are not self-conscious but Christ-conscious. They may not have the faintest idea what some one-off remark or gesture will have achieved.

Nor is there any special visible clothing that identifies the follower of Jesus! We have no distinctive head-gear and no particularly required diet. The Christian is not linked to any one region or culture of the world; there is no localised shrine to which we are obliged as pilgrims; we

---

2 Hession, p. 84.

have been given no official language for formal worship, and our prayers were never intended to be set recitations, to be learnt and pattered out.

The 'vision' that the Apostle Paul embraced – and shared with his readers in Ephesus – was of the unique Man of Eternity – appointed to bring all things in heaven and on earth together in Himself. Paul's words should be committed to memory by those aspiring, not after an 'it', but rather – 'Him':

> 'He who descended is the very one who ascended higher than all the heavens, in order to fill the whole universe' (Eph.4:10).

Here, in these few words, the *'one-ness'* blueprint has been stamped upon the vast system around us because of Christ, very God and very Man.

This is why we live, not in a *multiverse,* but in a *universe.* Through God in Jesus Christ, one mighty truth undergirds everything. Indeed, when learning centres were first set up in Britain and America, they were called 'Uni-versities' ... from two Latin words: *Uni* – 'One' and *Veritas* – 'Truth'. They were centres for the study of The One Truth. These were communities where everything you learnt stemmed ultimately from the one God and the one unchangeable truth in Jesus that holds everything together.

Of course, there were different chapters in this one, over-arching story. At university you could study physics, mathematics, music or philosophy – but these were all seen as slices cut from the one cake. The founding of most of these universities came out of a thoroughly Christian outlook. Thus, at Cambridge University, I was a member of Emmanuel College. Nearby was Christ's College, Jesus College, Trinity, St. John's, Corpus Christi and Magdalene.

It is only embarrassment at the name of Jesus and all He stands for that has caused certain universities now to adapt their original mottoes to something less obtrusively Christian.

Sure, today across the West, a massive loss of confidence has resulted in a wide and fragmented collection of different and irreconcilable belief-systems; '*Your*' truth, '*My*' truth; the Feminist story, the Marxist story, the Sexual-revolution story. Indeed today we are faced by the same world-view that confronted Paul and his friends – *the multi-faith story* that dominated all Europe in his own day.

Result? We now have around us a generation of ex-students, possessing degrees and PhDs – but many of whom are unable to give a credible explanation of the meaning of life on this world.

Paul's insistence was that Europe's array of gods and ever-competing platforms of thoughts had to give way to something far bigger, in that '*All things, in heaven and earth together, are to be brought under one head, even Christ*' (Eph. 1:10).

Once this stupendous objective is taken on board, the unity and meaning of our one short life become clear at last – even to a child of ten.

LIVING LIKE JESUS CHRIST

Simply to grasp something of the character of Jesus is to realise that nobody ever lived as He did. It is this recognition that inspired God's saints – Augustine and Jerome, Francis of Assisi and Patrick of Ireland; not to mention Kate Booth and Hannah More; R.A. Torrey and John Stott – with their single lifetime desire to become more like Jesus.

They – with Bible readers across the world – had joined hands in a common desire expressed by Paul: '*Be completely humble and gentle; be patient, bearing with one another in love. Make every effort to keep the unity of the Spirit through the bond of peace*' (Eph. 4:3).

Was that right? ... *Humble?* In Paul's passage, the scholars tell us that the word for 'humble' in the Greek original only took on today's attractive meaning with the coming of Jesus. Until then, the Greek word for 'humble' was equated with 'weakness'. And indeed, we will not find 'humility' among the qualities listed as desirable in job adverts today! 'Humble' to those early Greeks had that negative and mean – even cringy – feel to it.

But not after Jesus... . The Sermon on the Mount – 'Blessed are the Meek' ... the Last Supper – as He washed the disciples' feet ... then on the Cross – 'Father forgive them.' It is to Christ – the world's universal model – that we owe the positive and welcome meaning now widely attached to the word 'humble'.

When people truly live like Jesus, their neighbours and workmates cannot but take notice. This is where the power lies! When many *together* live in the Spirit – across social or denominational barriers – the power is multiplied sensationally. In a letter to a friend, the hymn-writer John Newton wrote, 'When a house is on fire, Churchmen ... Dissenters ... Methodists ... Moravians ... Mystics – all are welcome to bring water!'

The power of a life-style modelled on Christ leads us to the testimony of a businessman called Chris. He had been a con-man for years. His story was later made public. His was a cleverly thought-out plan of deceiving companies, and removing great sums of money from them without their ever knowing. Then, at a certain point, he would move on to another town, and perpetrate the same exercise again. By the time he had reached Norwich, in the English county of Norfolk, he had perfected the ruse.

It was then that he became attracted by the outlook and lifestyle of two students living nearby; they were members of Holy Trinity Church, where my brother-in-law, Gordon Bridger, ministered. Chris found himself restlessly drawn to the holy winsomeness of his Christian neighbours. One day he stopped them in the street.

'I see you go to that place down the road on Sunday evenings,' he ventured. 'Could you get me a ticket for tonight?'

The students refrained from correcting his ignorance of church – and intuitively responded, 'OK, Chris, we'll see what we can do!'

The morning passed – and the invitation was given: 'Hi – it's all fixed for tonight! We'll pick you up at 6.15, and take you with us.' Chris became nervous, but the two got each side of him and marched him into church. Gordon Bridger was preaching.

A little over an hour later, Chris emerged – as a Christian believer. His joy was unfettered. It was only later that – in a surge of guilt, and with a desire to make restitution – he confided in Gordon as to his criminal activities. Eventually the police were brought in and Chris confessed all. Yet after thorough investigation he was informed that he had evidently covered his tracks so successfully that none of the defrauded companies had realized what had transpired under their employee – and no charges were made. From that moment on Chris was a freed man.

It only takes an unobtrusive life in which Christ has the central place, and – whatever our limited ability with words, Bible verses or gospel language – the Spirit of the Lord will be at work. He can be trusted to open 'windows' of opportunity, as were simply opened for the two Norwich students.

Then I think of Lilian Clarke – referred to earlier. Deeply touched as she was by the revival in Africa, it is truly hard to think – apart from her professional teaching aptitudes – where her spiritual 'gifts' lay. But she was loved by the revival brethren, for she unconsciously radiated the Lord whom they also knew.

We came to know Lilian well, when she 'retired' from service in Uganda. Yet – on returning there for a brief visit – she was visited one Saturday morning by the elders of the nearby Kabale Cathedral.

'Miss Clarke, we would very much like you to preach for us in the cathedral tomorrow morning.'

Lilian drew back, appalled. 'Oh no, no,' she insisted firmly. 'I'm not a preacher; I don't preach! And indeed, I'm hesitant – as a woman – that I should even think of preaching for you in the cathedral.'

Deflated, the elders acquiesced. 'Very well, but we're sorry that this cannot be.' They left.

That evening, they showed up again. 'Miss Clarke, sorry to bother you – *but we disagree* with your earlier decision that you will not be preaching tomorrow morning. Please reconsider! You will know what to say!'

Lilian still demurred. 'No, truly, this really is not going to be possible. Thank you for your dear trust – but I will be glad to come and simply be with you all in church.' This seemed to be the final word.

Next morning, on arrival at the cathedral, Lilian was met by the elders at the gate: 'Good morning Miss Clarke: praise the Lord! You will be preaching this morning; everything is ready for you!' And preach she did – in the local Lukiga dialect.

'Begin it in me,' we will sometimes pray. The old prayer across many generations has so often been 'Oh God, send a revival, and begin it in me.' Roy Hession – and William Nagenda – would immediately have questioned that word 'it'. Of course we fully echo the prayerful desire for a World Awakening – exercised by millions on every continent. Half nights – and even whole nights – of prayer are held for this purpose – and the reason is obvious, when we consider the darkness that envelops great swathes of society. As long ago as 1969, the historian, Arthur Bryant wrote,

> 'Can all the King's horses and all the King's men put Humpty Dumpty together again? It is anybody's guess. But, short of a world-wide religious revival to evoke the selfless and cooperative qualities inherent in men, I can see no other way in which the disruptive and destructive forces threatening to tear Western materialism apart can be withstood.'[3]

Aleksandr Solzhenitsyn was of the same mind, in his Templeton Award address of 1983, in London, when he declared, 'Today's world has reached a stage which, if it had been described to preceding centuries, would have called forth the cry, "This is the Apocalypse."'

But – it's not an 'it' we are seeking … if it is, we will never find it.

---

3 Arthur Bryant, *The Lion and the Unicorn* (London: Collins, 1969) p. 306.

While continuing to pray that the current awakenings in numbers of countries will spread, the soil upon which an awakening can descend needs to be prayerfully and obediently prepared. The many human examples given in this book have shown us the way; true and practical Repentance as a way of life; daily Submission to the Lordship of Jesus as we read and understand His Word; and the daily Opening of our hearts to the Spirit's fullness, leading to the outward sharing of our gifts and blessings.

'One loving spirit sets another on fire' was Augustine's explanation of the early blazing spread of Christianity.

It's not *'it'* – but Christ Himself. Consider again the width of His world embrace!

> 'He who descended is the very one who ascend-
> ed, higher than all the heavens, in order to fill the
> whole universe' (Eph. 4:10).

We may ask how can one person fill the universe? The answer must be, that there is no part of the universe that is beyond Christ's reach and rule. No power anywhere can claim, 'Well, He can't touch us.' Ah, but He can; He will – and He does!

Further, if one Man fills the universe, it can only mean that there is no room for anybody else! Paul and his colleagues had the confidence to insist that every other deity and ideology would have to move aside, *because Jesus has taken all the space.* Lastly, if one Man fills the universe, it also means that we live, not in a Christ-deserted world, *but in a Christ-filled world.* That inspires us never to write off any country, any heathen opponents, dictatorships or terrorist regimes.

In the brimming, Spirit-filled world fellowship that is ours in Jesus Christ, we must see to it that we work *together* for our turbulent world. For when a house is on fire, all are welcome to bring water!

We are to be like David of old, in 2 Samuel 5:24; ready to detect *'the sound of a going in the tops of the mulberry trees'* – with its alert that God, in His reviving power, is on the march! Then is the moment to 'bestir ourselves,' as we march with Him. The prayerful waiting will be over, for – as the Africans will be saying – 'The rains have come!'

> *And it won't be long*
> *It won't be long ...*

A PRAYER

God our Heavenly Father, dear Lord Jesus Christ, blessed Holy Spirit, I come this day to You, the glorious Trinity. Awaken my soul to the angelic music of Heaven, where the morning stars sing together, and the sons of God shout for joy.

As for me, O Lord, graciously blot out my transgressions according to Your covenant promise, that my sins shall be remembered no more. Create in me a pure heart, and renew a steadfast spirit within me. I bless Your name, dear Lord, for the triumph of the Lion of Judah who, with His Blood, purchased us for God, from every people and nation. Let me abide in Him this day and take my part as one of His faithful witnesses in our turbulent world.

Let me claim His gracious promise that He and the Father will come and make their home with those who love Him. May I be filled with the Spirit of truth and grace this day, and be Your loyal steadfast ambassador wherever I go and to all I meet.

Amen – Come Lord Jesus!

EQUIPPED
TO SERVE

RICHARD BEWES

Richard Bewes was born in a missionary family on the slope of Mount Kenya, attained a degree from Ridley Hall Theological College, Cambridge, and worked in Christian ministry until his retirement in 2004. His ministry in south-east England led to his post as the rector of All Souls Church in London for twenty-one years. What makes a Christian worker? What does it mean to give your life to Christian work? *Equipped to Serve,* is an answer that was built from a lifetime of ministry.

ISBN: 978-1-78191-286-7

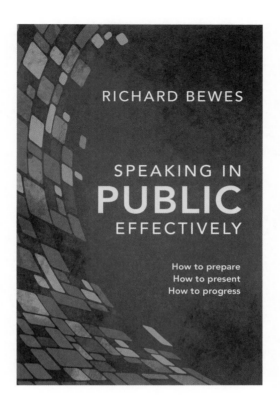

If speaking in public is normally something that concerns you, or fills you with fear, then this book will leave a warm rosy glow on your cheeks and the irresistible urge to try some of the ideas out as soon as you can. Richard Bewes, with deep knowledge and careful insight, carefully divides up the subject into easily digestible sections in a way that is memorable, and sprinkles anecdotes about his own experiences to illustrate many points.

ISBN: 978-1-78191-683-4

RICHARD BEWES

THE
LAMB
WINS!

A Guided Tour Through the Book of Revelation

'Makes Revelation leap to life and relevance.' DON CARSON

What is the average person to make of the book of
Revelation, with its vivid imagery and its apocalyptic
visions? Richard Bewes steers his readers through the
minefields of controversy and bizarre interpretations.
He picks out the great themes and landmarks that are
the message of Christ to every generation of believers.

ISBN: 978-1-85792-597-5

Stephen Olford writes, 'Never was a church-wide, heaven-sent revival needed than at this present time. It is the only answer to the spiritual warfare we face in every part of the world. Bombs, bullets and body bags will never stem the tide of terror and horror that threatens human existence. We must recognize that "the weapons of our warfare are not carnal but mighty in God for pulling down strongholds, casting down arguments and every high thing that exalts itself against the knowledge of God, bringing every thought into captivity to the obedience of Christ" (2 Cor. 10:4-5).'

ISBN: 978-1-84550-075-7

Christian Focus Publications

Our mission statement –

STAYING FAITHFUL

In dependence upon God we seek to impact the world through literature faithful to His infallible Word, the Bible. Our aim is to ensure that the Lord Jesus Christ is presented as the only hope to obtain forgiveness of sin, live a useful life and look forward to heaven with Him.

Our books are published in four imprints:

CHRISTIAN
FOCUS

Popular works including biographies, commentaries, basic doctrine and Christian living.

CHRISTIAN
HERITAGE

Books representing some of the best material from the rich heritage of the church.

MENTOR

Books written at a level suitable for Bible College and seminary students, pastors, and other serious readers. The imprint includes commentaries, doctrinal studies, examination of current issues and church history.

CF4•K

Children's books for quality Bible teaching and for all age groups: Sunday school curriculum, puzzle and activity books; personal and family devotional titles, biographies and inspirational stories – because you are never too young to know Jesus!

Christian Focus Publications Ltd,
Geanies House, Fearn, Ross-shire,
IV20 1TW, Scotland, United Kingdom.
www.christianfocus.com